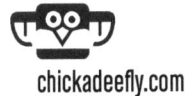
chickadeefly.com

Logo Identity Crisis

Finding soul in simplicity

A business leader's guide to a logo you love

Written and designed by
Lorelei Grazier Danilchick
linkedin.com/in/loreleidanilchick/

Copyright © 2026 Lorelei Grazier Danilchick
All rights reserved.

Published by Chickadee Fly Press
Killington, VT

ISBN: 979-8-218-87900-6

All rights reserved.
No part of this book may be reproduced, stored,
or transmitted in any form or by any means, electronic
or mechanical, without prior written permission of
the publisher, except for brief quotations used in reviews
or critical works.

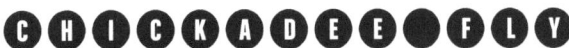

Typeface credits

Baskerville, originally designed by John Baskerville in the 1750s, was one of my earliest type loves.

ITC New **Baskerville**, purchased from *MyFonts*, is used for the main copy and chapter quotes.

According to *Fonts In Use*, ITC Baskerville was designed by John Quaranda. Several sources say it was released in 1982 based on the 1978 revival by Linotype, which was in turn a revival of the 1932 Monotype version by George W. Jones. This is unconfirmed.

Matthew Carter is also credited to this design, but some sources say he was only responsible for the Greek.
I do love Greek food and anything designed by Carter.

Gotham was designed by Tobias Frere-Jones with Jesse Ragan and released in 2002. I chose Gotham for subheadings, lists and side-notes because it contrasts Baskerville, is easy to read and has a bold spirit. It fit the bill perfectly, and I adore it.

Chalet Comprime is the Chickadee typeface used for the name when combined with the logo. It is also the display type featured within the circles: on the cover, inside cover, the table of contents and on page xii for 'NO SNOBS'. Its condensed form has strong personality and contrasts beautifully with the bulbous circles. Chalet was created by House Industries in Rhode Island, a remarkable type foundry whose work is well worth exploring.

DEDICATION

To Prof. Michael Graham
and Prof. Charlotte Story

Thank you for believing I could be a designer before I even understood that it was an option.

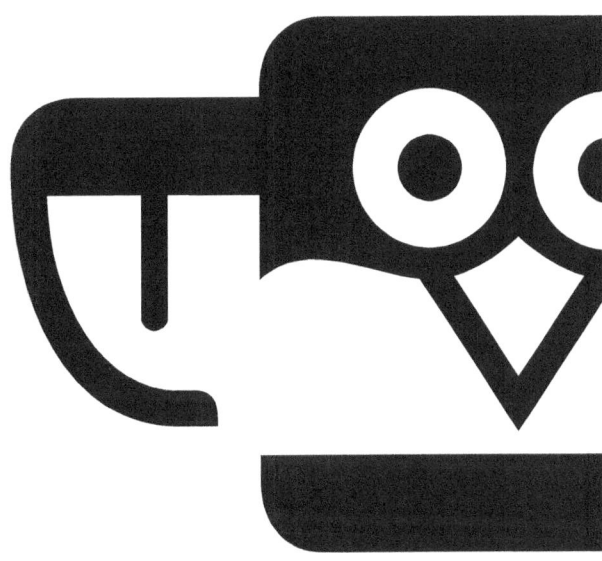

Good design is good will

"Design, good or bad, is a vehicle of memory. Good design adds a value of some kind, gives meaning, and, not incidentally, can be sheer pleasure to behold; it respects the viewer's sensibilities and rewards the entrepreneur. It is easier to remember a well-designed image than one that is muddled.

A well-designed logo, in the end, is a reflection of the business it symbolizes. It connotes a thoughtful and purposeful enterprise and mirrors the quality of its products or services. It is good public relations – a harbinger of goodwill. It says, 'We care.'"

Excerpt from *Design, Form and Chaos* by Paul Rand, American art director and graphic designer, famous for corporate logo designs, e.g. IBM, UPS, Westinghouse, Morningstar, ABC.

Thank you, Paul Rand, for your thoughtfulness and your contribution to design. The world is a better place because of you.

Finding soul in simplicity.

Table of Contents

● ● ● ● ● ● ● ● ● ● ● ● ● ● ● ● ● ● ●

Foreword by Paige Arnof-Fenn viii
A Message to Clients ix
Introduction x
Who is this book for? x
What's in this book? xi
Logos xi
Disclaimer: No snobs allowed xii

Chapter 1: About Logos 1
What is a logo? 2
What makes a good logo? 2
What makes an exceptional logo? 2

Chapter 2: Different Types of Logos 4
Pictorial, Brandmarks 4
Case Study: Shell 7
Letterform Marks 8
Case Study: Univision 9
Wordmarks 10
Case Study: Coca Cola 13
Case Study: The Gap 14
Brandmarks, Abstract 15
Case Study: AT&T 17
Badges, Emblems 18

Chapter 3: Stay, Tweak or Change 20
Stay 20
Tweak 21
Change 21

Chapter 4: Choosing a Designer 22
Hiring a designer 23
When AI is your designer 24
Can you copyright an AI generated logo? 25
AI is not going away 26

Chapter 5: Working with a Designer **27**
Design instincts 27
It takes two to tango................................ 28
Client questions..................................... 29
The creative brief................................... 30
You can't please everyone 31
Example: National Nonprofit....................... 32
What to expect in a presentation.................... 32
Example: Outline for my logo presentation......... 33
What if I don't love the logos presented?........... 33

Chapter 6: Money Matters **34**
Lets start with some logic 34
Good, fast and cheap? 35
Example: AmeriCane 36
Small Business Association (SBA).................... 38
Consider your competition 38
Pride in your graphics............................... 38
Designing merchandise 38
Case study: The Black Dog 39
Investing now or later?.............................. 39
Do you value design, personally?.................... 40
Budget constraints and creativity 40
Example: Reconnect Hungary 41
Case study: Morningstar 42
Why is this logo worth so much?..................... 43
Example: Hannibal's Coffee........................ 44
Straight talk for clients............................. 45
Example: Highland Mountain Bike Park 46
How much does a logo cost? 48
Why pay a premium? 48
Logo fees.. 49
Famous logos and their fees......................... 50

Chapter 7: Empowering the Client **52**
Problem... 52
Objectives... 53
Process 54

Conclusion: Finding Soul in Simplicity............ **58**

Gratitude **59**

Foreword

Your logo is more than just a graphic. It's your company's signature, your story at a glance, and often the first impression your audience will ever have of your brand. Get it right, and your brand can become unforgettable. Get it wrong, and you risk being just another commodity in a crowded market.

I learned this early in my career at Procter & Gamble, the company that pioneered modern brand management and built some of the world's most iconic and beloved brands. Later, at Coca-Cola, I worked alongside top creative talent with budgets that allowed us to craft brands recognized across the globe. Those experiences taught me one thing: strong branding isn't a luxury; it's a necessity.

When I founded my own marketing firm more than 20 years ago, my mission was simple: bring world-class marketing and design expertise to organizations of all sizes, especially those with a vision to make a difference. Every organization deserves the right words and visuals that tell their story with clarity, emotion, and impact.

That's why I'm thrilled about Lorelei Danilchick's book. Like me, Lorelei had exceptional training before she started her firm, and her work reflects that expertise. She brings an uncommon blend of artistry, strategy, and heart to every project. This book is proof: it's approachable, practical, and packed with real-world examples that help readers truly understand what makes a logo, and a brand, successful.

Whether you're creating a new identity or refreshing an existing logo, this book is your guide. It will give you the insight and language you need to collaborate confidently with designers, champion great design, and elevate your brand. Consider this your starting point for building a visual identity that not only looks beautiful but also works hard for your business.

Enjoy the journey, you're in excellent hands.

Paige Arnof-Fenn, Founder & CEO
Mavens & Moguls
Because Marketing Matters™

A Message to Clients

When I was in design school, all I cared about was improving my craft. I sketched a cube for a year, explored daily in Weingart's Type Shop, and practiced calligraphy like it was my meditation. Any free time was spent on experimental photography, figure drawing, or reading about design legends. (Okay. Also ultimate frisbee and snowboarding. I'm human.)

What I didn't consider was you: the client.

I didn't realize you'd have your own design instincts, or that I'd need to sell my ideas. Years of training had sharpened my skills, and my ego, but it hadn't prepared me to communicate design to non-designers.

Why wouldn't every client immediately love and approve my work? (Eye roll.)

Though I was confident in my design skills, my early clients humbled me. My design-snob attitude was missing the point. For my designs to improve and be approved, I had to listen to non-designers. Your questions and suggestions taught me that I needed to progress my communication and presentation skills to a higher level. And yes, sometimes a design does need more work. ;-)

This book is for you. It offers a foundation in design. Not so you can become a designer, but so you can think like one. As you read, you'll start to see the world differently, sharpen your visual instincts, and, I hope, become a true design ambassador.

This book was inspired by business people who care deeply about their work, just like you.

Thank you!

ll.

Lorelei Grazier Danilchick (AKA: LL)
chickadeefly.com

> "Whenever you see a successful business, someone once made a courageous decision."
> — Peter F. Drucker

Introduction

Hiring a designer and approving designs takes courage. Your company's visuals create an impact when no human is there to speak for you. What visual voice do you want your company to have?

Who is this book for?
In this book, I am speaking to business professionals similar to those that I have worked with over the years: start-ups, small and medium business owners, strategic planners, and branding and marketing professionals. Like you, all of my clients excel in their profession. You are good at what you do. Now you want your visual brand to align with the value of your service or product. You need a graphic professional that can address your needs and your objectives.

> Creating a million-dollar brand before earning your first million is a great way to set the tone for your business.

The goal of this book is to increase your understanding of design and empower you to find the right designer for your business, someone you can trust and consider a partner who is invested in your success.

Some business executives have difficulty discerning between good and bad designs. They may be uncertain about how to hire the right designer, or if they are working with a designer, they feel uncomfortable making selections or approving designs. They may be confused, intimidated, inflexible or apathetic about the process.

My job as a designer is to help the client understand what I'm doing and why. I need to provide clarity that allows them to engage confidently. This enables us to have business conversations about design. A healthy client/designer relationship will uplevel everything.

What's in this book?
In this book, you'll read case studies and see examples to help you understand logo design.

Creating a million-dollar brand before you have earned your first million is a great way to set the tone for your business. Perhaps I can play a part in getting you there.

I provide examples of sharp business people working with talented designers, creating timeless brands. A few mishaps are exhibited to help round things out.

We will cover different levels of designer fees and what you can expect from each. More importantly, I will show what makes a good logo and why some logos do not function well. Real stories from my business are shared to help illustrate what works and what does not work.

Logos
Designing a great logo that is unique and has never been seen before is only half the challenge. The harder part is feeling confident in approving it. From Paul Rand I learned that a logo is, by nature, minimal: just a mark and a name. At first glance it carries no meaning, so it's natural to feel uncertain. A logo earns its meaning over time, and your role is to introduce it, stand behind it, and use it consistently. This book will help you take that leap of faith with confidence, so your logo, and your brand, can truly shine.

NO SNOBS

Disclaimer: No snobs allowed
This book is a friendly guide to help non-designers approach design with confidence and curiosity. You don't need funky glasses or a deep knowledge of typography to spot good design, you just need an open mind.

Be confident in your business, curious with your designer, and above all, enjoy the collaboration.

> "Extraordinary work is done for extraordinary clients"
>
> — Milton Glaser
> Renowned Graphic Designer

Chapter 1

About Logos

Though I'd like to say that the design alone makes a logo great, that would be wrong. You, the client, play a big role in making a logo great. Your product or service stands behind the logo and gives it meaning. You can hire a talented designer to create an amazing logo. If your company does not deliver, both will fail.

Since you're reading this book, you clearly care about every aspect of your company. You take pride in your product or service. You want a logo that captures your company's soul while differentiating you from the sea of competition.

> Corporate logos that express a brand's symbolic, functional or sensory benefits, have a significant positive effect on customer commitment to a brand.[1]

You want something memorable. You want a logo that does not have a shelf-life. No expiration date. Timeless.

Let's face it. It's cool to have a great logo. And it's lame to have a mediocre logo. (There, I said it.) Now let's get into what makes a logo.

What is a logo?
A logo is a mark that acts as a symbol for your company.

In the words of Paul Rand[2]

> A logo is a flag, a signature, a street sign.
>
> A logo does not sell (directly), it identifies.
>
> A logo is rarely a description of a business.
>
> A logo derives its meaning from the quality of the thing it symbolizes, not the other way around.

What makes a good logo?
Developing a good logo is a mix of art and science. The art comes from a designer's imagination and ability to create. The science comes from market research, functional studies and formal sketches.

> **Memorable** (recognizable at a glance)
>
> **Unique** (not confused with others)
>
> **Simple** (works at all sizes and in black and white)

What makes an exceptional logo?
Emotional connection.

That's the heart of a truly great logo. And it only happens when good design meets good business.

When people love your company, they become fans. And when they love your logo too, they wear it like a badge of honor—on laptops, car windows, toolboxes—proudly showing that your brand reflects their values. It makes them feel good.

A strong visual brand succeeds by serving its audience well. When the business delivers, the brand earns trust, and the logo becomes a symbol of that connection.

That's when momentum builds. Your logo starts showing up everywhere. In some cases, fans remix or reinterpret it. One of my clients, Highland Mountain Bike Park, told me about a fan who shaved the Highland logo into the side of their head. That kind of loyalty only happens when a logo is meaningful enough to become part of someone's persona and simple enough to replicate.

In *The Power of a Good Logo*[1], published by MIT Sloan School of management, the researchers found that corporate logos that express a brand's symbolic, functional or sensory benefits, have a significant positive effect on customer commitment to a brand, and thereby a significant impact on company performance in terms of revenues and profits. The research also indicated that separate visual symbols used as logos tend to be more effective than brand names at creating a sense of emotional connection with consumers.

Humans like pictures ;-)

The authors also argue that logos symbolize a brand's essence, thereby building closer relationships with customers, creating strong positive emotions and facilitating top-of-mind recall. That's a great reason to hire a good designer.

> I wanted to understand how companies like Apple and Airbnb managed to fully leverage the combined capabilities of Science, Technology, Engineering, Art, and Math in their products and services.
>
> What did I find?
>
> That design-infused companies fully understand how art is the science of enjoying life, and thus, in order for their customers to enjoyably live with their products, they need to involve artists in how their products were made.
>
> – John Maeda, *How to Speak Machine*

> "For every single design problem, there is more than one good solution, and many, far too many, bad solutions."
>
> — Prof. Michael Graham
> The American University

Chapter 2

Different Types of Logos[3]

Pictorial, Brandmarks
Recognizable Object

Looking at strong logo examples and understanding what makes them work helps us develop an eye for great design. It also helps to see logos that miss the mark. By comparing both, we can better understand what to aim for and what to avoid.

The World Wildlife Fund
Designed by the San Francisco office of Landor
Tom Suiter, Creative Director, Jerry Kuyper, Design Director,
Jenny Leigundgut, Primary Designer

Clear form. Recognizable. Lovable. (One of my favorites.) Landor hit it out of the park. The positive and negative space work together to create the form. "As I remember, our working attributes were: not too cuddly, not too ferocious, and most certainly, not about to go extinct." stated Jerry Kuyper.

When the WWF represents all animals, how can you use only one for the logo? You can. It is a symbol.

Chicadee Fly Design
Designer: Lorelei Grazier Danilchick

Bold form of a bird in the style of a totem. This insinuates the chickadee as a powerful spirit animal. The intent was to be fun and bold.

Beach Pea Baking Company
Designer: Lorelei Grazier Danilchick

An artistic line drawing of a pea pod with a nod to a loaf of bread. Though the form is a mundane object, the lines are exquisite and give it a feeling of lightness. It is meant to express the artistry of Beach Pea's baking. Afterall, it's not just a loaf of bread.

Early County 2025 (Georgia, USA)
Designer: Lorelei Grazier Danilchick

The inspiration behind this form was the magnolia flower. After many sketches, I honed in on four petals feeling like a compass, with one petal being different. In theory, this petal symbolized growth, change and moving forward. What matters is that the form is clear, unique, memorable and easy to reproduce.

NBC
Designer: Steff Geissbuhler at Chermayeff & Geismar

This mark not only illustrates a great use of positive and negative space, but also shows how one small part of the form can make a huge difference. The beak brings this mark to life.

Target
Designer: Inhouse

This is as simple as they get. Often non designers ask me what makes it so good? In my humble opinion, part of what makes this great is the bold step the client took to use such a simple logo AND then the follow-up designs that worked the logo into their greater brand strategy. *And let's not forget all the hard work the business teams have done over the years to ensure Target delivers.*

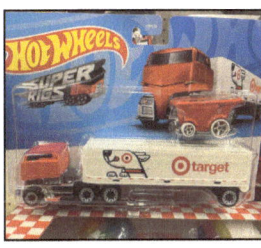

Recognizable at small size.

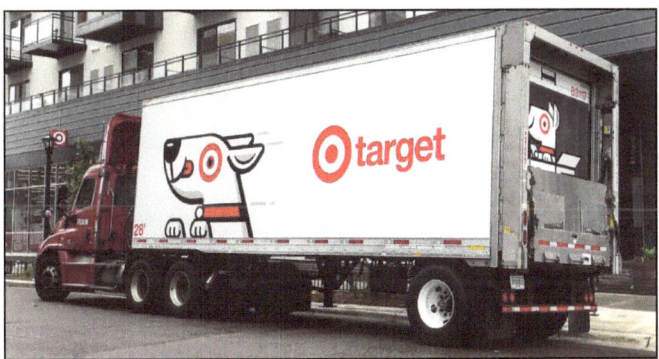

Simplicity of form brings more options.

What Not to Do
The examples below try to do too much. They're overly complex, hard to reproduce, and rely on color as a crutch. Strip away the color or the name, and there's nothing memorable left.

Even in today's vibrant, full-color digital world, a logo with true strength and impact should stand on its own, without depending on color.

Designers who create overly complex marks are often less experienced, trying to cram in too much meaning. They illustrate rather than imply. I made the same mistakes as a young designer. Sometimes a client dictates every detail, and the designer doesn't yet know how to explain why that's not the best choice. Don't be that client.

This level of design typically costs $50–$250. You are paying for computer skills rather than design sensibility.

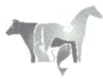 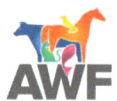

 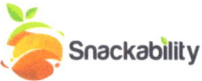

Color

SIDE NOTE

In the larger perspective of branding, color plays a powerful role. Color gives us one more clue to recognize a brand. It sets a tone and helps communicate meaning. The Target red and the color spectrum of the NBC peacock are significant. When you see a dark green awning, you might start craving a coffee.

Yes, color does matter. And remember that in symbol design, form comes first. A logo needs to be clear and effective without relying on color or scale. The clarity of the form will help make the color even more powerful. They work together.

CASE STUDY: Shell

Evolution of a pictorial logo

Shell's yellow and red scallop shell logo is one of the most recognisable symbols in the world, but it started life as a black and white mussel shell.[4]

The logo begins as an illustration and evolves to be more simple and iconic in form. Through use, the company realized that it was more recognizable from a distance when it was simplified. The transformation highlights a core principle of identity design: insinuate, don't illustrate.

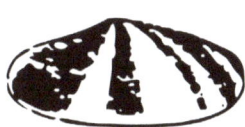
1900-1904

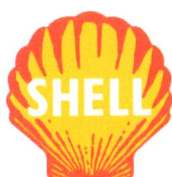
1948-1955

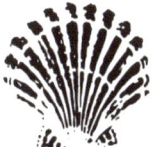
1904-1909

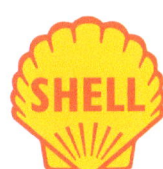
1955-1971

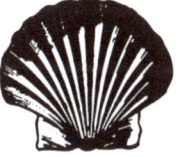
1909-1930

1971-1995

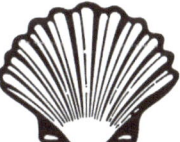
1930-1948

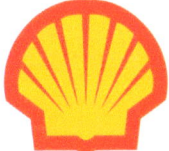
Current

Letterform Marks
Use a single letter as the logo.

Grazier Design Works
Designer: Lorelei Grazier Danilchick

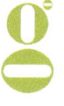

Three letter o's creates one letter g. It's fun to create something normal in an unusual way. This design was nominated for best logo design in the 2007 AIGA BoNE Show Awards. (Best of New England)

Highland Mountain Bike Park
Designer: Lorelei Grazier Danilchick

The stylized H form is inspired by the knobby wheels on mountain bikes. It plays with positive/negative space. The client dubbed this, *the invisible H*. One of my highest compliments came when a Highland fan shaved the logo on the side of his head. That requires a clear form.

Andrews McMeel Universal
Designer: Steff Geissbühler at Chermayeff & Geismar

At the core of Andrews McMeel Universal's publishing are humor and self improvement books. The addition of two eyes immediately turns the U letterform into a human face. The careful positioning and proportion of nose and eyes make the face versatile in that it is either humorous or plain, depending on the context.

Waypoint
Designer: Lorelei Grazier Danilchick

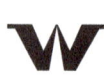

Waypoint is a real estate development company.
The bold mark insinuates direction. The inside of the W creates perspective, like a road or a tall building.

The Hired Pens
Designer: Lorelei Grazier Danilchick

The exclamation mark tells us something is important. It draws attention and insinuates a loud voice while the parentheses are used to make side notes and insinuate a softer voice. The Hired Pens can craft copy that draws attention without having to shout.

Rare Sportbikes For Sale
Designer: Lorelei Grazier Danilchick

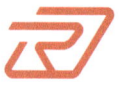

This website is for sportbike enthusiasts and collectors. The audience loves riding sportbikes fast and around corners. The form of the logo is inspired by the motoGP race tracks and it intentionally does not insinuate a specific make or model, as there are many.

What not to do

The examples below were taken from an on-line logo generator utilizing AI. The computer wanted to add character to the letters, but did not know how to do it without creating clutter.

1990 - 2012

Current

CASE STUDY: Univision

Is change always good?

The Univision logo, designed by Chermayeff & Geismar in 1990, is usually seen in color, yet it works in black and white. The simple shift in shape in the top left quadrant breaks the expected and gives the form life.

Univision is a window to the world. This idea, combined with a simple form that insinuates the letter "U" opens up a world of options. Simplicity brings flexibility.

Since 2012 the Univision logo has been redesigned twice. On the left you can see the latest iteration, and in my humble opinion, the updated logos are not as strong as the previous logo. However, the designers responsible for the redesign are talented and capable. Perhaps the client was pushing for the redesign? When executives want change, an updated logo can symbolize a shift.

Sometimes a logo update is necessary, and sometimes it is not. Hopefully this book will help you recognize a timeless logo vs. a trendy logo and help you decide if a logo change is really needed.

If the brand needs a refresh, perhaps it can be accomplished without changing the logo. See the simple update to the Virgin logo on page 21 or see how the Starbucks logo evolved on page 18.

Wordmarks
Use a word, name, acronym, or product name.

IBM
Designer: Paul Rand

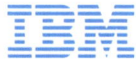

The IBM logo is a great example of a formal idea. When Rand designed this logo in 1962 the color blue and stripes were not associated with technology or business. He designed the letterforms; strong, bold and unique. Without the stripes, however, they were too heavy. The stripes enabled the logotype to lighten up visually while still remaining strong, they made the form more unique, and it gave Rand a design element (stripes) that could be used throughout the visual branding for IBM.

When Rand introduced the striped logo to IBM one executive said it reminded him of the Georgia Chain Gang. Thankfully that executive did not have veto power. Remember to be wary of opinions. Everyone has one.

Arabica
Designer: Lorelei Grazier Danilchick

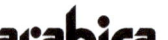

Arabica was designed while studying at the Basel School of Design. My objective was to create a word mark using the latin alphabet that insinuated the arabic alphabet.

Funky Wrap
Designer: Lorelei Grazier Danilchick

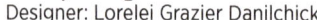
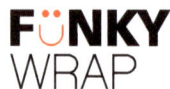

Funky Wrap is fun in a subtle way. The design needed to be clear enough to embroider on a small fabric tag. The original logo, on page 12, was far too complex.

503
Designer: Lorelei Grazier Danilchick

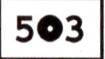

This logo mimics the product. 503 is a pinhole camera kit made of cardboard. The camera looks like a small box with a hole.

Crossroads Partner
Designer: Lorelei Grazier Danilchick

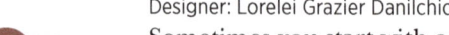
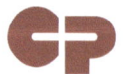

Sometimes you start with a concept and sketch to see if it works visually. Other times, like in this example, the idea reveals itself as you sketch. The plus-symbol/crossroads appeared naturally as I worked on the letterforms, and it just clicked into place.

Victoria & Albert Museum
Designer: Alan Fletcher

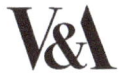

Great example of combining forms with minimal moves creating maximum impact. The cross-bar of the A is the serif of the ampersand. The letters are close enough to create a form of their own, while separate enough to be read quickly, V&A.

Citi Bank
Designer: Pentagram, Paula Scher

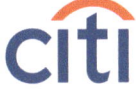

When Citicorp and Travelers Group merged, they asked Pentagram to create their new logo. Paula Scher famously saw the simple solution early, drawing it on a napkin at the kick-off meeting. The $1.5million[5] fee was not for her time, it was for expertise, experience and execution of the new logo across their whole company.

FedEx
Designer: Lindon Leader at Landor Associates

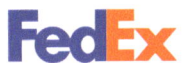

Federal Express was in business for over 20 years when they approached Landor for a redesign. This wordmark simplifed their name and their logo, bringing everything down to their core.

Asprey
Designer: Pentagram

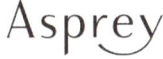

Asprey, a British luxury brand known for its jewellery, silverware, and leather goods, underwent a masterful redesign by Pentagram. The update modernised its visual identity for the digital age while honoring its heritage, striking a balance between tradition and innovation. This is an excellent example of how subtle typographic adjustments can elevate a brand without losing its legacy.

RbG music
Designer: Lorelei Grazier Danilchick

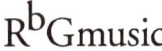

My brother, Russell Boyd Grazier, asked me to create a mark for his music composition work. I imagined this as something that could be letterpressed or stamped onto a music sheet hundreds of years ago. Timeless design is always the goal.

What not to do

The logos below may look passable at first glance, but neither holds up as a strong mark. Can you see how they fall short of being a strong logo? The Waypoint logo on the bottom left was utilised before hiring me (see the updated logo on page 8). This design is a composition with letters and shapes, not a clear mark.

The Lit Tech logo focused on the letters I and T, or is it supposed to be LT? The designer did try to make it unique, but the form is too busy. Do you need three circles? How much *swoosh* is needed to show the circles are orbiting the letters? Why box in the name?

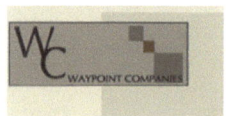

The designer for the original FunkyWrap logo, below, wanted to create something fun, which makes sense. He played with the word *fun*, chose a different fun typeface for *Wrap*, and used playful colors. A whole lot of fun was happening, but it lacked cohesion and never came together as a memorable logo. Simplicity and clarity were needed, along with fun.

The below right logo for Kisler, or Kistler, shows that the designer has an idea: incorporate a symbol for law (the scale) with the name. However, the scale interferes with reading the name. As a whole this design feels unprofessional – not the right look for a law firm.

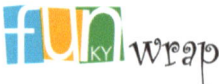   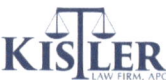

Often a designer has an idea, but does not know how to execute that idea into a clear logo. If the idea starts to interfere with the logo's functionality, the designer needs to recognize this and either change direction or figure out how to fix the issue. **The goal is always recognizable, memorable and unique.**

Chapter 2: Different Types of Logos

1886

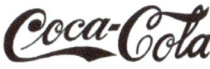

1887

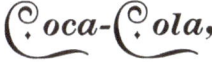

1889

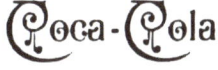

1890

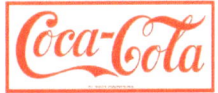

1891

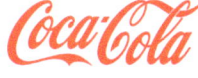

1941

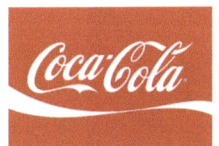

Current

CASE STUDY: Coca Cola

Evolution of a wordmark

The Coca-Cola logo was originally created by Frank Mason Robinson[6], the founder's partner and bookkeeper. His original design has endured for over a century and remains one of the most recognizable logos in the world.

Robinson hand-lettered Coca-Cola in Spencerian script, a popular writing style at the time, capturing the playful and effervescent spirit they wanted.

While the logo has evolved over the years, it has always stayed true to that original energy. The distinctive silhouette of the wordmark is recognized to the point where people see Coca Cola even if a different word is used or if it is written in a different language.

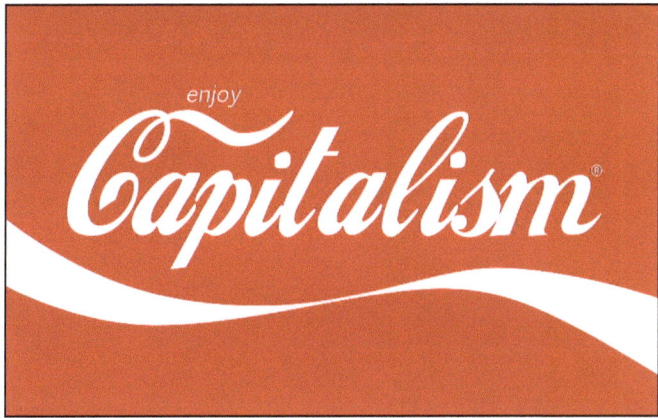

Below: Clearly, this is a Coca-Cola sign. Found in Disney World, using the Aurebesh alphabet from Star Wars.

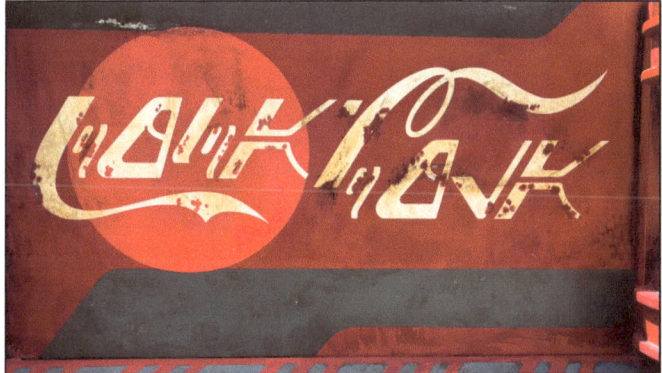

13

CASE STUDY: The Gap

Customer attachment to a logo

Stuart Crawford[7] shows how important it is to be in tune with your customers before making a change.

In 2010, Gap embarked on a bold endeavour to update its iconic logo, a decision that would ultimately prove to be a fleeting experiment. The intention behind this logo metamorphosis was to infuse the brand with a fresh and modern identity, keeping pace with the ever-evolving landscape of fashion and retail.

However, the redesigned logo was met with swift and vehement backlash from Gap's devoted customer base. The new emblem, characterised by its stark simplicity, failed to strike a chord with the individuals loyal to Gap for years. Instead of eliciting excitement and enthusiasm, the abrupt shift in branding left many feeling bewildered and alienated.

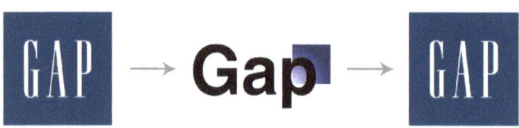

As a designer, I can tell if a logo has visual issues. As the business leader, you should be able to recognize whether the logo creates any strategic challenges for the company. For example: Is it too costly to reproduce? Too similar to another brand? Do your customers connect with it? Does it reflect your company's quality and values?

Sometimes a brand does need a full overhaul, other times it just needs a little tweaking. Try to be aware of how your logo is perceived by your audience. If they love it, but you are having challenges reproducing it, perhaps it may just need some minor formal adjustments. (See the examples in Chapter 3 on page 20.)

If you feel your visual brand needs a refresh, take a look at your full marketing strategy. Perhaps the logo could use some work, or perhaps other parts of your visual brand can be updated while your logo remains timeless.

Brandmarks, Abstract
A completely new form that stands on its own.

Chase
Designer: Chermayeff & Geismar

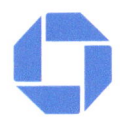

Originally designed in 1960, this mark has proven how a company can grow and transform while waving the same flag. There was inspiration for the mark and reasons for every formal decision. In the end it was a new and unique icon that people learned to associate with Chase. It is clear, memorable and unique.

ReConnect Hungary
Designer: Madison Eckley, Creative Director: Lorelei G Danilchick

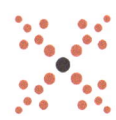

The Hungarian Human Rights Foundation (HHRF) needed a new logo for ReConnect Hungary, their birthright program. (Case study on page 52.) The new logo that you see here is clear, unique and inspired by the parent logo for HHRF which pulls from traditional Hungarian textile design. This modern simplification has the fresh spirit they wanted.

The Olympics
Designer: Charles Pierre Fredy de Coubertin

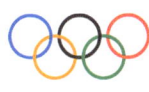

When I see the Olympics' logo, I feel my childhood dreams of becoming an Olympian. The logo represents more than the competitive union of elite athletes from five continents, it stirs up emotion.

AUDI
Designer: In house/unknown

The Audi logo is instantly recognizable, conveying prestige, quality, and status. Yet in the Chinese EV market, Audi replaced the symbol with a wordmark. Based on what I've outlined, this is a mistake. Symbols create stronger emotional connections, communicating the brand at a glance without reading. Considering the global recognition of the Audi rings, why discard them? CEO Gernot Döllner explained, "Chinese premium customers are different from their international counterparts and have different expectations."[8]

I have to wonder if this is the right move? Time will tell.

Note: The Olympics and Audi logos have similarities, yet we clearly differentiate the two. We do not confuse them because we have learned their meaning.

Project Zawadi
Designer: Carla Weathers, Creative Director: Lorelei G Danilchick

Using an abstract representation of the human form in a logo can be challenging. On page 8, Andrews McMeel subtly suggests a face without directly illustrating one.

While hand-sketching forms related to the letter Z, this sketch stood out. It evoked the image of a person with raised arms and it was recognizable, yet not too literal. It reminds me of hieroglyphics. It passed the test of being unique, simple and memorable.

What not to do
In a sea of abstract logos, many are overly complicated. The sheer number of poorly designed logos relying on abstracted human forms made this an issue worth calling out in this book.

Successful organizations focus on the people they serve. That doesn't mean a logo needs to include a literal human figure. If you're drawn to incorporating the idea or symbol of people, ask yourself: is it implied, or is it shown directly? Consider whether the form is simple enough to function as a logo while still carrying a distinctive, memorable character. Finally, ask whether it truly aligns with your brand strategy.

Examples of what not to do with the human form:

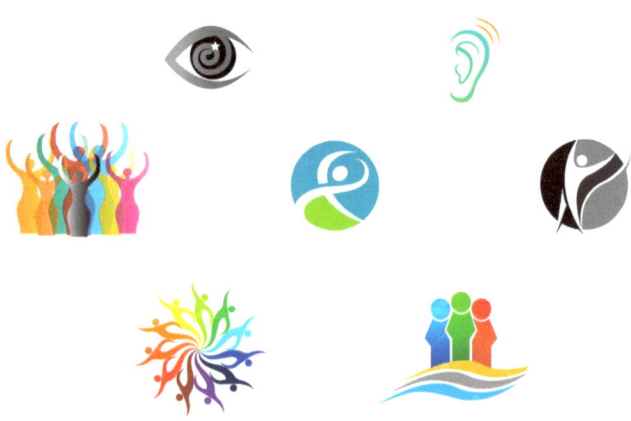

CASE STUDY: AT&T

Evolution from badge to pictorial to abstract
The American Telephone & Telegraph Co., AT&T, has had 11 logos since 1885[9]. In my opinion, 1969, 1983 and 1998 are the strongest designs.

1939

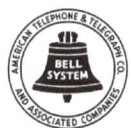

From 1885 to 1969, the AT&T bell symbol changed six times. Each version featured a black bell with lettering inside and around it (see example at left). The badge/emblem logo style was prevalent in the early 1900s.

1969

Saul Bass brought Ma Bell into the modern age with this pictorial icon. Look up "Saul Bass AT&T video pitch 1969". The video is an educational tool, showing the executives how this logo is more recognizable. He sold them the new logo by educating them.

1983

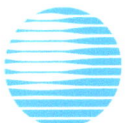

To mark a significant corporate restructure, Bass designed a new logo, breaking away from the bell. This new form insinuates global connectivity. This is a great example of a successful logo redesign. The business was making a huge change and the logo needed to reflect that.

1998

The globe was simplified by reducing the amount of lines and increasing their weight. This small tweak makes it more recognizable at very small sizes, as needed for the flavicon of a website. Sometimes a tweak is needed.

2005

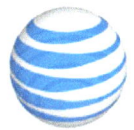

Corporate mergers and executive changes often bring new designs. At this time, many flat logos were getting updated to make them more dynamic. The added complexity of shading and layers makes this design weaker than the previous two logos. It has become more illustrative and less of an icon.

2015

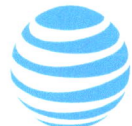

AT&T must have confronted issues with the complexity of the 2005 design as Interbrand collaborated with AT&T in-house to simplify the form. One can't help but wonder if the 2005 redesign was even needed?

Badges, Emblems
Name and symbol/shape combined to create a badge.

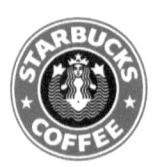

1971 Original Logo
Terry Heckler

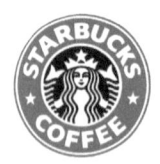

1987 Simplification
Terry Heckler

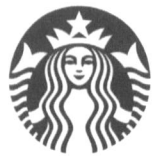

1992 Simplification
Doug Fast
Heckler Associates

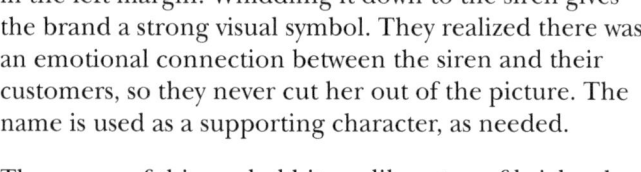

2011 Symbol Only
Connie Birdsall
Lippencott

Badge/Emblem logos are controversial. We love them for nostalgia, but they do not function as well as a symbol.

Seeing the evolution of these three famous logos will help you understand the challenges that come with a badge or emblem logo. Note that Mini Cooper is the only one that kept their name in their logo, and that is probably because Mini is a four letter word. ;-)

In Alina Wheeler's acclaimed book *Designing Brand Identity*, she did not include Badges/Emblems for a reason. I include the option here since small businesses often use them. If you want to have a badge or emblem, be aware of the limitations and talk with your designer about how the logo can work across different mediums and sizes. Know what you are getting into.

Starbucks
Evolution of the Siren

Starbucks used an emblem until 2011. See the evolution in the left margin. Whiddling it down to the siren gives the brand a strong visual symbol. They realized there was an emotional connection between the siren and their customers, so they never cut her out of the picture. The name is used as a supporting character, as needed.

The power of this symbol hit me like a ton of bricks when I walked into the Metropolitan Museum in NYC and the below sculpture made me crave a latte.

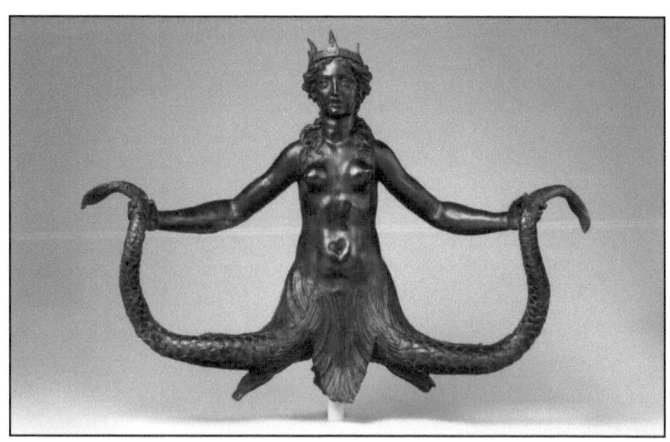

Anonymous, Siren, c.1571-1590, bronze, Rogers and Edith Perry Chapman Funds, 2000, The Metropolitan Museum, New York.

Harley Davidson
Designer: Inhouse

Harley-Davidson's classic badge logo, introduced in 1965, was recently simplified. The company kept the iconic shield shape, confident it's recognizable even without the name, and introduced a new wordmark and "H|D" letter-mark. Time will tell whether this modern approach can carry the same emotional weight as the original.

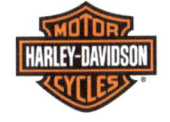
1965

2023

Harley's current challenge is attracting younger riders. The brand's heyday was rooted in 1970s chopper culture: leather jackets, loud bikes, and that bold, hard-to-read badge. It became iconic because it embraced rebellion and freedom. As trends changed, Harley felt pressure to evolve. The rebrand reflects that tension between staying true to its heritage and remaining relevant.

Mini Cooper
Designer: Inhouse

When the new Mini was first reintroduced by BMW in 2001, the influence of their history was clear. Now, as you can see on the left, it has been simplified.

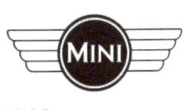
1968

In summary

As you look through the examples of good design, you may notice that logos come in many forms. Some are bold, others delicate. Some feel playful, others serious. A logo reflects your organization and speaks to your customers. It is never arbitrary.

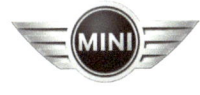
2001

Successful businesses use their logo as a keystone for their brand, experimenting with its formal attributes while maintaining a consistent voice. Coca-Cola has built equity in the swish of its letterforms, the contour of its iconic bottle, and, of course, the color red. Target also owns red, yet no one confuses the two. That's worth considering as you develop your visual brand.

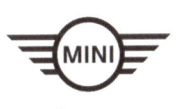
2018/current

Ask your team: How can we use our visual cues consistently without becoming predictable?
How can we express our core values in design?

You can train people to recognize your brand through the repeated use of key elements; logo, color, and type. Study brands that have mastered this, then look at your own. Above all, enjoy the process with your designer. Have fun with your brand and don't be afraid to explore.

"Only the wisest and stupidest of men never change."

— Attributed to Confucius

Chapter 3
Stay, Tweak or Change

When AT&T went global in 1983, a full logo redesign made perfect sense. Sometimes that's exactly what a brand needs. Other times, the heart of the logo is strong, but a few smart tweaks can solve functionality issues. And then there are cases, like The Gap, where the best move is not to touch the logo at all.

Trends will always come and go. The real question is: how do you know when your logo is evolving in the right direction, like Shell's on page 7, and when are you falling victim to a trend?

1969

Stay
Back in 1999, Burger King fell victim to *the millennium swoosh trend*. At the turn of the century, many brands felt pressure to make their flat, two-dimensional logos feel more dynamic. The solution, for better or worse, was often a swoosh.

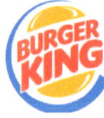
1999

One critic even nicknamed it the *toilet bowl effect*, since it looked as though logos were being flushed into a swirl. It's a perfect reminder that trends can quickly date a brand, while timeless design always holds up.

2021

In 2021, Burger King's classic logo returned, thanks to Jones Knowles Ritchie's careful refinements that honored the original design. This logo could have 'stayed' in 1999 or made minor 'tweaks' while the graphics used for ads and packaging could have taken on the trends of the day. Personally I'm grateful that they found their way and I am hoping they create merchandise that screams Americana in the best way possible.

Tweak

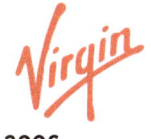
1978

Virgin wanted a logo that conveyed it's punk personality and would work for all musicians, while being dynamic and endurable. Cooke Key collaborated with a young calligrapher, Ray Kyte, in 1978 and created the scrawled script that defines the brand to this day.[10] The power of the name and spirit of the company are celebrated in this hand-drawn script.

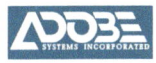
2006

Left is an 'update' from 2006. You might not even notice that it changed. Considering the strength of the original logo, Virgin kept the design in tact, making minor tweaks. The g and n are more legible and minor details in the line quality and spacing improved recognition at a glance. Smart move Sir Richard Branson.

Change

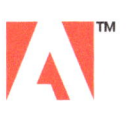
1982

In 1993, 11 years after its founding, Adobe changed its logo. Many companies rebrand after 5-10 years into business. At this point, the company has matured. They better understand who they are and what customers they want to attract. The original graphics may no longer represent the business properly.

Although there have been some modifications to the Adobe name since 1993, the lettermark remains. That is over 30 years strong for a logo. Well done!

1993

What makes the Adobe lettermark so good?

> You can reduce it to a small size, and it's still recognizable.
>
> The form is unique.
>
> Great use of positive and negative space.
>
> The form is timeless. It does not fit into a trend.
>
> The form feels appropriate for a creative technology business.
>
> The simplicity of the form gives it versatility.
>
> It works in black and white.
>
> And yes, the company delivers what it promises.

> "You must choose, but choose wisely."
> — The Grail Knight
> Indiana Jones, The Last Crusade

Chapter 4

Choosing a Designer

Hopefully, you now have a better understanding of what makes a good logo and what makes a bad logo, and are ready to start looking for a designer. Knowing that you've poured countless hours into mastering your expertise, what type of design professional will deliver at the level you deserve?

Considering the vision you have for your business, how much do you want to invest in your brand identity?

Whether you hire an experienced designer, partner with a boutique agency, turn to a family member with artistic talent, crowdsource on a budget, or use AI to generate your logo, each path produces a very different result.

A logo designed for $250 will not deliver the same level of thought, craft, and refinement as one created by a designer charging $8,000 or more. And while AI tools can generate a logo quickly, they lack the strategic insight and emotional resonance that a skilled designer can provide.

Be clear on what you value. If your goal is to have a distinctive, memorable identity that captures your company's soul, your expectations should align with your investment. In branding, as in business, you get what you pay for.

Hiring a designer

1. Review the Portfolio: Style & Versatility
Every designer has a unique style, and the best ones adapt to different brand personalities. Look for a portfolio that shows range—from bold to minimalist, across various industries. Versatility signals that the designer can bring your vision to life, not just their own.

2. Industry Experience—Or Not?
This depends on your preference. A designer with experience in your industry may understand your competitive landscape and audience more quickly. That can be helpful. On the other hand, a great designer with strong range can bring a fresh perspective that sets you apart. Don't discount someone just because they haven't worked in your exact field.

3. Creative Process & Timeline
Design is a process. Ask the designer how they work:

Do they begin with discovery sessions? Do they present multiple concepts or a single refined direction?

A clear, structured process reflects a thoughtful, client-focused approach. There's no universal "right" way. Find a process that suits you.

Requesting a timeline with milestones helps you understand your role in the process and gives insight into the designer's process.

On page 52, I share my own logo presentation outline. It helps clients feel confident and ready to have meaningful conversations about design.

4. Look for Testimonials, Recommendations & Referrals
Referrals from people you trust are gold. Past client testimonials also reveal how the designer works, communicates, and delivers. You want someone who listens, shows up, and follows through. If they've done it for others, they'll likely do it for you.

5. Budget
In chapter 6, Money Matters, we explore the typical range of design fees. This will help you set realistic expectations, choose the right designer for your needs, and invest wisely in your brand.

Final Thoughts
Choosing a logo designer is an important decison. Take your time, ask questions, and find someone who aligns with your vision, values—and yes, your personality.

You'll be working closely together, so it helps to genuinely enjoy the collaboration. A great working relationship can make the process not just more effective, but more fun.

When AI is your designer
It's time to address the elephant in the room: AI. It began quietly entering the design world around 2010 and became a major talking point by 2021. Since this book focuses on the formal side of logo design, I'll show you what happens when an AI-powered logo generator is asked to design a logo for Adobe.

AI Logo Generator
Name: Adobe
Industry: Software

AI kicks things off by showing you a flood of logos and asking which ones you like. There's no talk about your competitors, no digging into strategy. It's like a design vending machine pulling ideas from its massive database. After that, it has you pick a few words from a preset list to describe your company. And in less than five minutes, voilà: a shiny lineup of logos.

But here's the real question: Are any of these logos truly ready to represent your brand? Or do they still need the eye and expertise of a professional designer? AI is already a powerful tool and it will only get better. However, some businesses will know that they need a human touch in order to achieve an emotional connection between their visual brand and their customers.

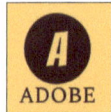 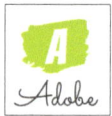 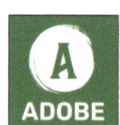 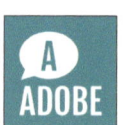 
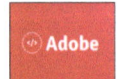  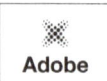 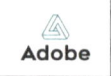 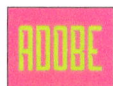
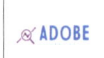 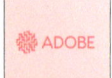 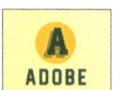 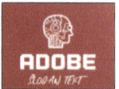 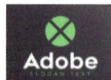
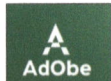 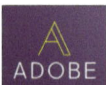 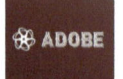 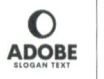 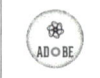
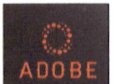 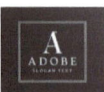 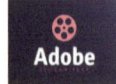 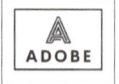 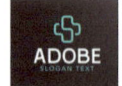

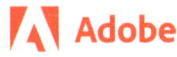

By now, you can likely see the difference between the AI-generated logos and Adobe's actual logo in the margin to the left. While some AI sketches show promise, a human designer is essential to refine ideas and ensure they align with your brand strategy.

> AI pulls from trends and common design patterns. This can leave your logo looking generic, trendy and weaken your brand's credibility.

Can you copyright an AI generated logo?
Right now, you can trademark a logo made entirely by an AI logo generator, but you can't copyright it. That means you're allowed to use it, but you won't have exclusive rights. Someone else could use the same design.

If, however, a human designer uses AI as a tool (say, to help with sketching ideas) but makes the key creative decisions along the way, that logo might be eligible for copyright. The U.S. Copyright Office reviews all cases individually to decide if there's enough human creativity involved, or not.

Excerpt from a 2025 report by the US Copyright Office[12]

The use of AI tools to assist rather than stand in for human creativity does not affect the availability of copyright protection for the output.

Copyright protects the original expression in a work created by a human author, even if the work also includes AI-generated material.

Copyright does not extend to purely AI-generated material, or material where there is insufficient human control over the expressive elements.

AI is not going away
We all know you can't stop progress. AI is here to stay, so the question becomes: how can we use it to strengthen our businesses, and create a better future? Right now, I see AI as an assistant. I can run ideas through it, but I can't get lazy. I must be the critical and creative human guiding the process.

Recently I saw a meme that said, "AI won't replace you, it will replace mediocrity." I took this to mean that we must strive to be great at what we do. We have to think beyond the universal brain of AI.

> 60% of consumers avoid brands with outdated or unappealing logos.[11]

Design is about more than generating shapes. A skilled designer makes deliberate choices about hierarchy, color, contrast, line quality, harmony and more. A designer with a strong business sense goes further, aligning those formal decisions with a brand's mission and values. And lastly, there is the element of surprise. Eurika! When an unexpected idea surfaces from the sketches, or a mistake turns out to be an interesting direction to pursue. AI is a powerful tool, but it won't catch the unexpected.

> "A horse designed by committee is a camel."
> — Hungarian Proverb

Chapter 5
Working with a Designer

Be confident with your business and curious with your designer. If a design feels intimidating, that's okay. You can ask questions and try to understand it more. After being curious first, not reacting out of fear, decide if it's going in the right direction for your company or not.

Design instincts
My friend Dr. Kristina Lamour, EdD, Professor of Design at Lesley University, often talks about design instincts. She once pointed out that every time we choose an outfit, we are making design decisions. (Duh. Why didn't I think of that?) Still, having an eye for design usually comes from exposure. Some people grow up surrounded by good taste; it's part of the air they breathe. The rest of us develop it through deliberate effort, by visiting museums, reading books, flipping through magazines, and training our eyes to notice what works. Some of us even spend a small fortune in art school refining those instincts.

Early in my career there were times when a client's design instincts took over the presentation and the project went off-course. This could have been avoided had I prepared a more thorough presentation. After repeated arbitrary comments like "Change the color to purple or add a swoosh." I needed to elevate my presentations or I would be doomed to mediocre design.

Paul Rand famously delivered a 100 page presentation to Steve Jobs for the NEXT logo. He educated the client. Rand did this because it made his job easier. He did not want to have to sell the logo in person. He wanted to inform the client so that they would 'get it' and then approve the design without hassle.

Professor Michael Graham at The American University, one of my first design mentors, blew my mind when he informed me that there can be multiple good design solutions to one design problem. I was sure that there was only one good solution and my job was to find it. (Yes, I often put that much pressure on myself.)

He continued to inform me that for the multiple good design solutions possible, there were many, many, far too many bad solutions that make it to the public domain.

Often I would wonder as a young designer, *how can so much bad design exist?*

SIDE NOTE

- Your designer will light up when talking about type.
- Offer to edit a design with your pdf editing software and watch your designer cringe.
- Designers are often a bit odd... maybe a lot odd.
- Your designer will care deeply about 1/16 of an inch.
- If you find a designer that shows passion-projects, like holiday cards, probono clients or fine art, then you know this person is a designer because they love working with visuals. This is a clue. They care.

It takes two to tango
According to Bob Gill, renowned Graphic Designer, "I've never had a problem with a dumb client. There is no such thing as a bad client. Only bad designers."

Well, that is an extreme statement and it made me think. Blaming bad design on the client always seemed weak. It's an excuse. How can I do better?

When a client is not clear on their business vision, they may struggle making design decisions that reflect their business. If you are feeling unsure about choosing a design, first establish a clear problem to solve. Have you and your designer set parameters to follow? Do you have a specific objective to guide the process?

> 75% of consumers recognize a brand by its logo.[11]

Perhaps you should craft a creative brief (see page 30) and use that as a guide throughout the project.

Another famous designer, Saul Bass, worked with the client to find 5 unique traits that described the company. While sketching ideas for the logo, Bass used the five words to critique his work. All viable logo options aligned with the 5 words.

Let's all avoid mediocrity. Good design requires the designer and the client to be good dance partners.

Client questions
Clients should never feel insecure making design decisions. Part of my job as a designer is to help you understand our world. You do not have to understand it at my level, just as I do not need to understand your business at your level. But you should feel comfortable asking questions and making decisions.

Client questions can be a catalyst that takes a design idea to a higher level or deepens your understanding.

Before you hire a designer or start a design project, ask yourself what you're trying to achieve from a business perspective. What problem needs to be solved? What is the end goal? Your business goal will help you find the right designer for the job.

The creative brief

A creative brief serves as a roadmap, aligning the client and designer to collaborate effectively and create a successful design.

As a tool, it can be helpful as you build a relationship with a new designer. You might not need these briefs as your relationship grows with your designer.

Sample Outline for a Creative Brief:

1. **Title and Description**
   Give the project a name, and a brief description

2. **Goals and Objectives**
   Define the specific business need and what the work will accomplish. What does success look like?

3. **Audience**
   Who are you trying to reach?

   List as many demographic specifics as possible and add what your audience values, wants or needs.

4. **Messaging and Tone**
   When your audience receives the message, what should they think, feel, want, and do?

   Think of your message as a person. It should have a voice (a personality) and a tone (a mood or attitude).

   Follow the company's brand guidelines to ensure the tone and voice of your messaging matches that of your overall brand and keeps you consistent across marketing initiatives.

5. **Decision Makers**
   Who is involved and what role do they play? Be clear about roles, responsibilities and who gives the final approval. You and the designer need to know who has the final word. That is the only person that can sign-off on designs.

SIDE NOTE

Who is God?
Paula Scher, Award Winning Designer and Partner at Pentagram, said at an AIGA conference on Business and Design that she asks the client, "Who is God?".

Who has veto power? She wants to avoid getting approval from one person, only to learn later that there is a higher-up that does not approve of the work.

Be clear about who has decision-making power and then stick to the plan.

6. Assets and Deliverables
What will be the final work? Will it be a logo with brand guidelines? An advertisement? Be sure to include details like the medium, dimensions and amount of deliverables.

7. Budget
Establishing a budget not only helps everyone stay on track and keeps the project sustainable, it can also help the creative process. Constraints bring insights and inspiration that can help enrich the project. In Chapter 6, page 40, I give an example of how budget constraints can lead to creative solutions.

8. Timeline
Creating a timeline during the proposal stage is helpful. Clients do not always understand the steps needed to create good design, and we must allot time for approvals and revisions. Mapping out a timeline helps establish the pace of the project, and sometimes it reveals that this is a rush job, which will change the cost and put a fire under the team to stay on target.

9. Distribution
How will your audience see the work? Map out how and when the new logo/identity will take over the old. If a small business can't afford to replace everything all at once, there can be a plan of attack that meets the budget and strategically gets the new image out over a period of time.

You can't please everyone

I was once hired by someone in the HR dept of a large organization. She wanted me to help the company incorporate art and inspirational quotes into the interior design of the headquarters. This was a purposeful job that excited us both. As we moved through the process, she started inviting more people into the conversations and asking more people for advice on the designs and artwork. In the end, the project fell apart.

> 23% revenue increase is linked to consistent logo use across platforms.[11]

At the very beginning I could have set the boundaries. Now I know. And now you know. Don't be that client. Don't let a great project fail by trying to please everyone.

> **EXAMPLE: National Nonprofit**
>
> **Too many options**
>
> A friend was working for a national non-profit in the middle of a rebranding project when she called me to help her and the CEO choose a design direction.
>
> To my surprise, the design firm had sent them about 50 sketches to review, with no recommendation or presentation. The CEO could tell the designs were subpar, but my friend didn't realize the poor quality. She felt overwhelmed by so many options and she needed guidance.
>
> **The designer should guide you**
>
> If you're unsure about making design decisions, ask your designer questions and request a recommendation. Have them explain why a particular design will work and show examples of how the logo could be applied.
>
> In this case, the design firm had experienced web designers, but no one had worked with logos. Everyone assumed the logo would be easy, probably because they look so simple!

What to expect in a presentation

A logo presentation can make or break a project. It's the first moment everyone sees the work, and excitement runs high. That's why I take the time to research, sketch, refine, evaluate, reflect, and make sure every detail, from legibility to strategic thinking, is carefully considered.

I usually send the presentation 1–2 days before our meeting. This gives you a chance to absorb the ideas, without the pressure of having me in the room. Often, seeing something new can be surprising, and this time allows you to process it so our discussion is focused, productive, and even fun.

The best part? Hearing a client say, "That's not what I was expecting, and I love it!"

> **EXAMPLE: Outline for logo presentation**
>
> 1. Clearly state the problem we are solving, including variables, mandatories and end goal. Approved at kick-off and used to guide the sketching.
>
> 2. Educational section showing what makes a good logo and what makes a bad logo. Relevant examples are best. My clients always appreciate this section.
>
> 3. Glimpse into the process showing decision-making. Discarded sketches show why decisions were made and how the logo evolved.
>
> 4. Clearly present 1 to 3 viable logo options. This number is not a set rule. The designer should decide which sketches work and only present those. You should not be innundated by too many options. An experienced designer will guide you.
>
>   If one design is recommended over the others, the designer should show clearly why.
>
> 5. Illustrate logo usage in sample applications. This will help you understand how well a logo functions.

What if I don't love the logos presented?
This happens. Be confident in your business vision, and inquisitive with your designer. Ask questions with an open mind.

Consider revisiting the creative brief (see page 30). Perhaps there was a misunderstanding, or some main points were not addressed.

A healthy conversation can lead to understanding. Your questions might shed light on something that was not discussed in the kick-off meeting. Your questions could help propel the process deeper or pivot the direction. Or, you might get onto the same page as the designer. Questions bring clarity.

In my experience, when clients are given a thorough presentation that educates them, they show up to the meeting with a decision made excited to move forward.

> "Good design is good business."
> — Thomas Watson Jr.
> Former President, IBM

Chapter 6

Money Matters

With small and medium-sized businesses, the budget often becomes a block. It seems easy for big corporations to hire expensive design agencies and create great work, but what about smaller companies? Does it make sense to invest in design?

Design matters if you want to get the most out of your business. The question is, how much should you budget?

Logo design services are advertised on the web for under $100. Large design agencies can charge over $100,000. Where do you fit in?

Let's start with some logic
A small local bakery can crush it with a great location, amazing products and good customer service. One could even argue that all it needs is a superb product, and success will come. The bakery might not even have a logo. It may have a sign that the local sign company made without any strategic thinking into the visual brand. Of course, they would benefit from great design, but one could argue that it's not as important for the small local bakery as it is for the start-up skincare line that will be on the shelf, competing with all the other skincare products. This is logical.

Good, fast and cheap?
You can have it fast, you can have it good, you can have it cheap, but you can only pick two. This should fall under logical as well.

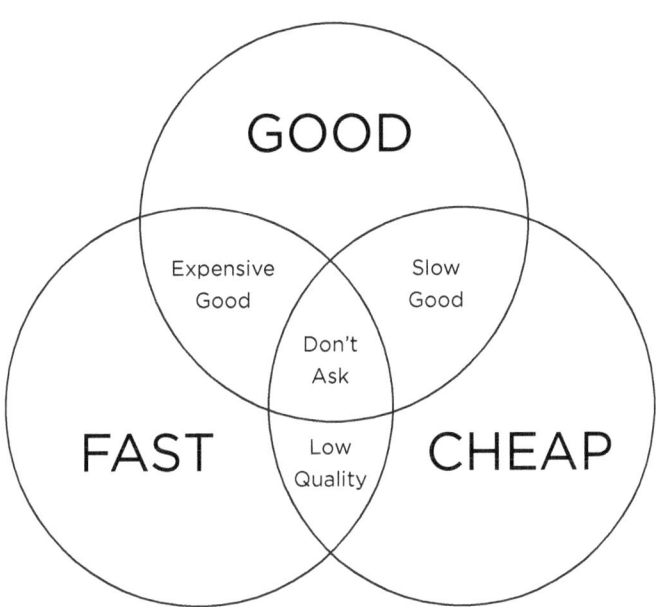

You can have it fast and good, but it will not be cheap

You can have it fast and cheap, but it will not be good.

You can have it cheap and good, but it will not be fast.

77% of marketing leaders say a strong brand is critical to their growth plans.[13]

EXAMPLE: AmeriCane

Fast and good, not cheap

AmeriCane needed a new design for their wholesale sugar bags and they needed it fast. There was no time for revisions. The client trusted me completely. They provided the content from the old bags and emphasized that warehouse workers needed to recognize each type of sugar at a glance.

That was my creative brief.

With just a weekend to develop concepts, I sketched multiple ideas on Friday, revisited them with fresh eyes on Sunday, and refined the strongest concept. By Monday morning in the studio, I had selected the Pantone colors, finalized the artwork, and submitted it to the client.

After the initial bags were printed and it was time to expand the range of sugar types, the client suggested adding more elements, but this design thrives on simplicity. Less really is more.

The project went on to win the Biannual AIGA Best of New England (BoNE) design award in the packaging category. Due to this high recognition, the client framed and proudly displayed the bags in their office. The design became a conversation starter during sales meetings, showcasing both the variety of sugar they offer and the care they take in producing it.

This project reinforced something I have seen time and again: recognition amplifies pride. Great design energizes employees, sparks conversations, and opens doors.

AIGA 2009 BoNE Award Winner, Packaging Design

Not a logo project, but it was *fast*.

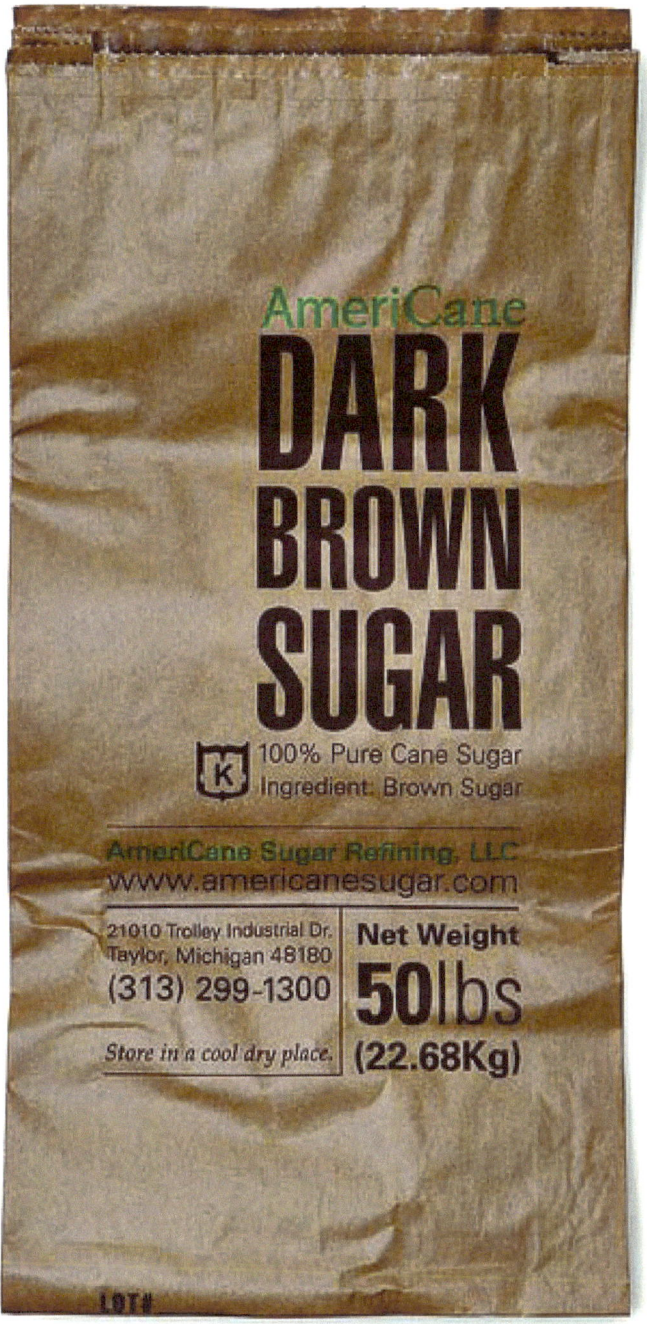

Small Business Administration (SBA)
According to the SBA, small businesses and startups with revenues less than $5 million should spend 7-8 percent of their revenues on the marketing budget. This budget can include logo design along with advertising, website, social media, direct mail, events and much more. You and/or your marketing professional will know what type of marketing is best for your business and good design can amplify any marketing plan. (I hope you become a design ambassador and look for ways to incorporate good design into everything you do.)

Consider your competition
Are you in a highly competitive market? If so, you will need to invest in your marketing strategy and design to stand apart from your competitors. Effective design will bring a marketing strategy to life.

If you're not in a highly competitive market, ask yourself how you want to show up in the market. Do you want to stand out? Maybe you can spend less on traditional advertising, get your message out with social media marketing which is cost-effective, and invest in kick-butt design to make that message memorable.

Pride in your graphics
When your sales team loves your website and all the materials you provide, they sell with energy and enthusiasm. It's like the difference between heading out on a date in a stylish outfit that flatters your physique and expresses your personality, versus wearing clothes that don't fit or reflect your vibe. In the first case, you walk out the door confident and excited; in the second, you may feel apprehensive and want to hide.

Designing merchandise
If this bakery becomes successful and has a following of loyal customers, there is a market for merchandise. This is one of the many ways great design can help a small business. A well-designed logo that can be printed onto shirts, hats, aprons and stickers can not only bring in more revenue for the bakery, it can also help get new customers as the loyal customers wearing the shirts are walking billboards.

> **CASE STUDY: The Black Dog**
>
> **The power of a symbol**
>
> Off the coast of Massachusetts, on a small island called Martha's Vineyard, sits The Black Dog Tavern. Over time, it built a second business around its brand. The story goes that visitors loved the tavern so much, they began asking for the cooks' shirts. That sparked the beginning of their merchandise line.
>
> It's important to note: people loved the tavern first. No matter how iconic a logo may be, if it represents a bad experience, no one will want to wear it.
>
> What if the logo hadn't featured that simple black dog? If it was just type, or an unappealing symbol, would the shirts have become so popular? In my opinion, no. This is a perfect example of a clear, memorable symbol, the black dog, paired with a positive, authentic experience.
>
> **The Black Dog brand hits a trifecta:**
> 1) the beloved tavern, 2) the iconic black dog symbol, and 3) the charm of Martha's Vineyard.
>
> People connect with all three. Now, The Black Dog merchandise has taken on a life of its own—so iconic that people buy it even if they've never set foot on the island.

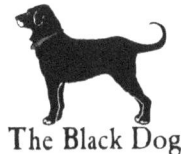

Investing now or later?
Do you want to start strong with a custom design or save that level of branding for phase two? The bakery example could use the first five years to get its system down, build a solid team and create community awareness through word-of-mouth, joining the chamber of commerce and participating in local events.

Once the bakery is established, perhaps they start catering or sell baked goods online. As the business reaches more people, visual branding helps with recognition and customer satifaction. Receiving a box of cookies in a well designed package that aligns with your brand and feels like a treat will bring emotional connection and a desire to share.

Perhaps, as in the case of The Black Dog Tavern, people love the bakery and the town it's in. In this case, the bakery merchandise serves as a souvenir.

As you saw on page 21, Adobe refreshed its design 11 years after launching. Morningstar Investments updated its logo 8 years after starting (see page 43). Many of my clients come to me after 5–10 years in business, when they realize they've outgrown their initial logo. They've proven their ability to succeed, and improving their visual brand helps take their business to the next level. It's never too late to elevate your image.

Do you value design, personally?
Some people care about how they show up in the world. They feel that first impressions matter. These people will likely care about the aesthetics of their business as well. It's okay for your reason to come from the heart rather than be backed by business data.

Steve Jobs knew he wanted the Macintosh computer to have font choices because that mattered to him, and on a gut level, he knew it would matter to others. Up until that point, nobody had access to different fonts.

The team working on the original Macintosh did not understand Jobs' obsession with fonts. Your business partner might not understand your desire for great design either. Your CFO might not understand. You get it. Perhaps this book will help you state your case.

Budget constraints and creativity
Early in my career I listened to an interview with one of the Monty Python creators. He told the story of the coconuts. You see, in *Quest for the Holy Grail,* King Arthur's servant used coconut shells clapped together to sound like horses. It is truly absurd, memorable and hysterically funny. The coconuts helped create an iconic scene.

So why did they use coconuts? How did some creative person come up with that idea?

Budget. Monty Python could not afford horses. How can King Arthur and his loyal servant travel the countryside on horseback, without horses? Coconuts, of course.

That story puts my mind in the right place every time I see budget as a constraining variable in a design problem.

EXAMPLE: Reconnect Hungary

Good and slow, affordable fee

The Hungarian Human Rights Foundation (HHRF) realized that the logo for their star program was not living up to the quality of the program itself. They also recognized that it was not aligned with the young audience they wanted to attract and it did not have a connection to the parent logo for HHRF.

Reconnect Hungary is a Hungarian Birthright Program and after 10 years running, the positive impact that this program has on preserving Hungarian culture around the world was clear. So the leaders of the HHRF wanted to redesign the logo for Reconnect Hungary and give it the proper visual branding that it deserved.

HHRF is a small non-profit with small budgets, however, the board recognized the importance of the logo so they called me and we negotiated. (Besides having a weak spot for logos, I also have a weak spot for Hungarians. I lived in Hungary from 1992-95 and I fell in love with the country.) With the help of a junior designer, I could do the job within their budget, as long as the timeline was cushy enough for me to take a young designer through the process and avoid stress. ;-)

BEFORE

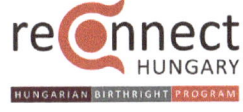

AFTER

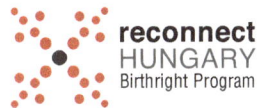

Inspired by traditional textile design, this modern simplification is the fresh spirit they were seeking. More details in Chapter 7 on page 52.

If you have an overall marketing budget for launching your business or helping your business get to the next level, partnering with a smart and creative designer can help you maximize that budget.

Designers feel a demented bliss when confronted with a creative challenge.

Paying for a high level designer can bring savings in other areas. And more importantly, the work done will have more impact, bring more results and be more lasting through time.

> **CASE STUDY: Morningstar**
>
> **Investing big and early**
>
> As recounted by Barbara T. Armstrong in *Good Design Is Good Business. Just Ask Morningstar* (Forbes.com), the story of Morningstar's logo is a testament to the long-term value of great design.
>
> In 1984, Joe Mansueto founded Morningstar in his Chicago apartment. Today, it's a global financial services powerhouse with over 10,000 employees. But back in 1991, just eight years into the business, Mansueto made a bold and strategic move: he invested in a logo.
>
> Recognizing that a strong visual brand was essential for a growing company, he paid $50,000—no small sum at the time—to commission legendary designer Paul Rand, known for iconic logos like IBM and ABC. Hiring Rand, the éminence grise of corporate identity, was a defining moment for a young company—and it has since become part of Morningstar's origin story. To this day, Mansueto considers it one of his smartest early business decisions.
>
> As stated by Don Phillips, president of Morningstar's Investment Research division:
>
> *Any company placing major emphasis on what can be measured will inevitably underestimate design—since it's not easy to measure.*

Why is this logo worth so much?
Can you see why the Morningstar logo is good design?

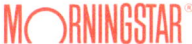

Often simplicity is confused with ease. People see a clear mark like Morningstar or IBM and they think anyone can do that. In reality, years of training and critical thinking enabled Rand to create a logo design that looks simple.

Rand was given a long name to work with. Morningstar is 11 letters long. While he was sketching the type, looking to create unique letterforms that could become a signature, he explored how an image could be incorporated with the type in an effort to give it a more unique silhouette and to insinuate meaning.

> The cost-benefit payoff [for design] is very, very high, but I can't give you a specific number or way to measure it.
>
> – Joe Mansueto, *Morningstar Chairman and CEO*

When you glance at the Coca Cola logo type, you do not have to read it. You recognize it because of the unique silhouette. With Morningstar, Rand created condensed type so that the logo could be reduced to small sizes, and instead of the letter O keeping with the condensed typeface, he pushed it out wide to break the rhythm and insinuate the rising sun. (The sun is a star.) This one formal shift does two things; it helps give the logo type a unique silhouette that can be recognized at a glance, and it insinuates meaning without being literal.

Can you see the mix of art and science here? The science is readability and recognizability. The art is in the rising sun. Rand could have put a star shape in place of the O, he could have added sun rays to illustrate that it clearly is the sun, or he could have just used the non-condensed O to break the rhythm. He pushed the design further to see how he could keep it simple enough to work, while being interesting and unique. Tah dah!

EXAMPLE: Hannibal's Coffee

A logo that creates money problems

Hannibal's Coffee Company was a well-funded start-up in 1995, aiming to compete with Starbucks. To make a strong first impression, they hired a renowned design firm with an impressive portfolio. The resulting logo, however, was beautiful but not functional.

The design was a detailed painting of an elephant in front of a mountain range—created by an artist who also painted posters for the P.T. Barnum Circus. While it would have made a stunning wall mural in a café, it failed as a logo. A logo is a mark, not a painting.

Logos must work in one color. If you take away only one lesson from this book, let it be that. Simplicity enhances recognition and versatility—no matter how big your company is or how much money you spend.

When Hannibal's tried to stamp the intricate logo onto coffee bags, the details were lost, leaving a smudged, ugly mess. By then, the company had already invested in large back-lit signs and other applications using the logo. They needed a redesign that would simplify the mark while preserving its essence, allowing them to keep all of their signage.

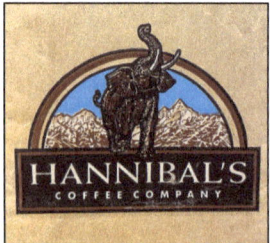
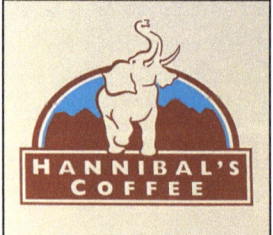

Before: Smudged art and details are lost.

After: Simple shapes and clear lines.

Straight talk for clients

I don't know what happened during the original design of Hannibal's logo. Perhaps the designers presented strong concepts, but the client chose a painting instead. If so, that choice created challenges: it was expensive, difficult to reproduce, and ultimately led to wasted time and resources. The company then came to me to address the problem.

That said, I'm not suggesting designers are always right or that clients should follow their lead blindly. This book exists because of what I've learned from my business clients. You're smart, and your insights matter. The key is to avoid dictating design decisions. Instead, create a dialogue and let your designer apply their expertise.

82% of investors want the companies they invest in to have a robust brand.[14]

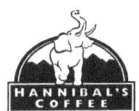

My work for Hannibal's was a fix. It solved their business problem and functioned effectively, but it wasn't the great logo it could have been. I was glad to help, but I would have preferred a full creative exploration from the start, uncovering the logo's full potential.

EXAMPLE: Highland Mountain Bike Park

Investing big and early

The founders of Highland Mountain Bike Park set out to create something special. A park built by riders, for riders. It was their first time building a bike park, and because they were the target audience themselves, they knew exactly what would make it great.

They also noticed something about the places they loved to visit. They always left with a shirt featuring a cool logo. When it came time to launch Highland, they brought me in to design an identity that riders would be proud to wear—something that said, *I've ridden here*.

The logo's stylized H draws inspiration from the knobby wheels on mountain bikes, playing with positive and negative space to create a bold, memorable mark.

More than 15 years later, that original logo is still going strong. As one Highland rider told me, "When I see a Highland logo, I know that you are family."

This is the power of thoughtful design + good business.

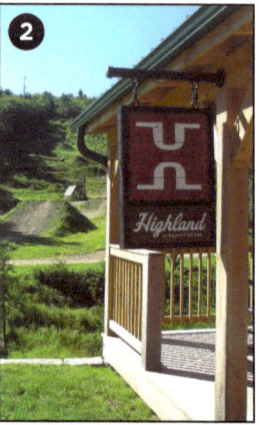

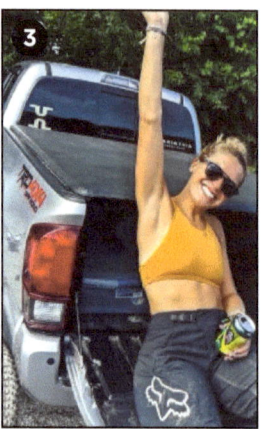

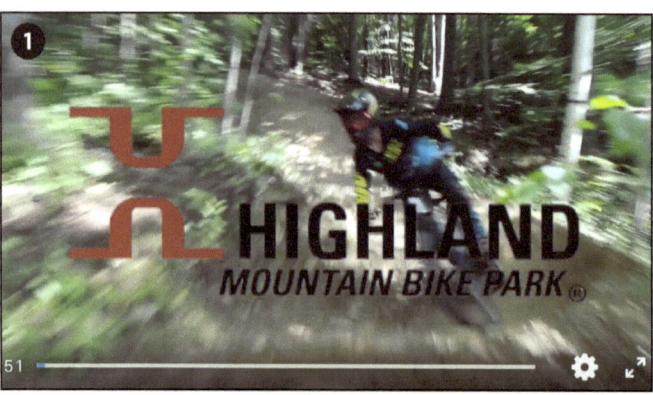

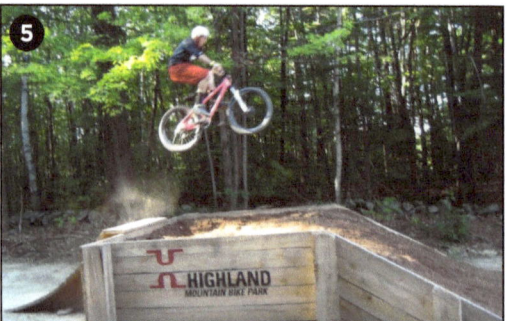

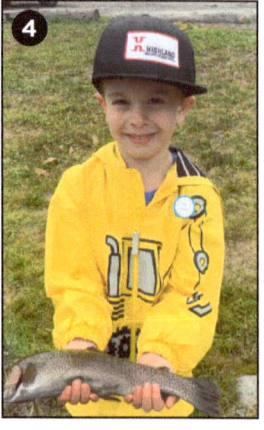

1) Branding YouTube videos.
2) Wood cut signage.
3) Alex co-branding Highland with her Toyota.
4) Highlanders go fishing too.
5) Simple enough to stencil.

Chapter 6: Money Matters

6) Simple enough to stencil. 7) Chris sporting Highland while skiing 8) James said his Highland shirt was his favorite birthday gift. 9) Highland sticker on a ski tuning machine in Killington!

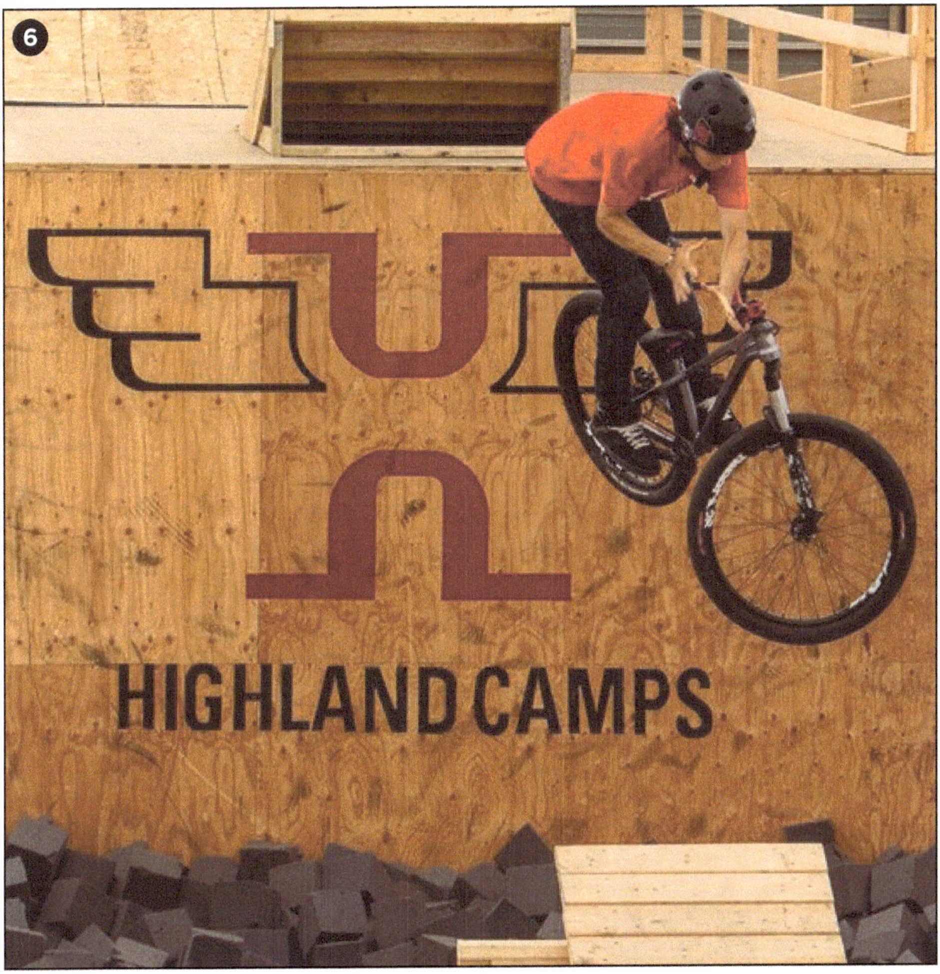

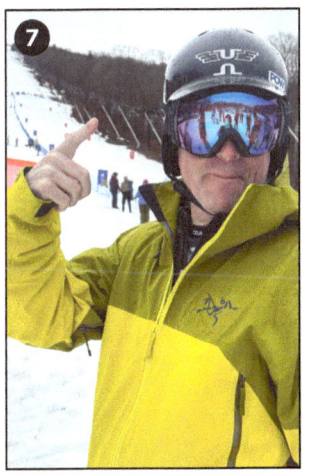
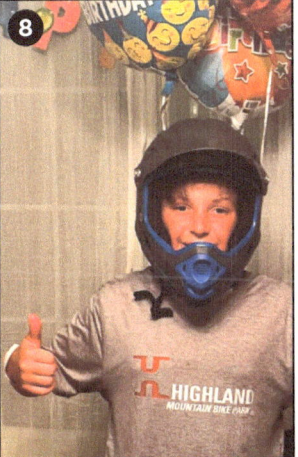
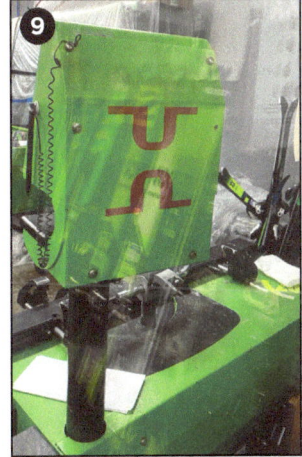

How much does a logo cost?
Custom design is just that, custom. The price depends on two main things: the size and potential of your business, and the experience of the designer.

To prepare a quote, I look at the project as a whole: the scope, complexity, and the impact the design will have. That means asking questions like: Who is your competition? Are you B2B or B2C? Local, regional, or national? Planning to grow? Who is your audience?

These insights help me create a logo that works strategically for your business and is priced fairly for the work and value it delivers.

Why pay a premium?
Your logo is more than a graphic mark. It is a strategic asset that can influence brand perception, market position, and long-term business success.

A well-designed logo grows with the business. It scales, adapts, and maintains its integrity across formats, from social media to packaging to signage. Businesses pay more for something that will last and won't need redoing in a year or two.

> Logos need to make an impact within 2 seconds.[11]

As told by Mark H McCormack in his book *What They Don't Teach You at Harvard Business School*, in the section titled *Charge for Your Expertise*.

"It always reminds me of the story about the woman who approached Picasso in a restaurant, asked him to scribble something on a napkin, and said she would be happy to pay whatever he felt it was worth. Picasso complied and then said, "That will be $10,000."

"But you did that in thirty seconds," the astonished woman replied.

"No," Picasso said.

"It has taken me forty years to do that."

Logo fees
Below is a general breakdown based on my experience. Estimates typically include research, concept development, 2–3 viable logo options, two rounds of revisions, and a branding guide. Branding guides can range from a single page to 30+ pages, depending on the depth of documentation. Social templates, merchandise, websites, and other marketing pieces increase scope and can be added as line items.

Here is what you can typically expect at each level:

Budget: $500 and under
Crowdsourced platforms, AI-generated logos, or work by inexperienced designers. Strategy is minimal or absent, originality is limited, and brand support is minimal.

Low-Range: $1,000 - $3,000
Typically created by a newer designer building a portfolio. You may get a nice logo, but research and brand strategy are limited. May not include logo guide.

Mid-Range: $5,000 - $15,000
Experienced designer or small studio. Suitable for successful small businesses refreshing an original logo, mid-sized companies, or startups launching with a strong brand foundation. Will include logo guide.

Upper Mid-Range: $15,000 - $30,000
Experienced, award-winning designer or small agency providing a comprehensive branding guide and a more robust logo guide and brand system.

> 75% of consumers recognize a brand solely by its logo, emphasizing the importance of a memorable design.[14]

High-end: $50,000 - $100,000+
Renowned designer or established agency offering extensive strategy, stakeholder workshops, and a fully developed brand system.

Famous logos and their fees
All inflation calculated at usinflationcalculator.com

Morningstar: $50,000 in 1981[16] ($179,749 in 2026)

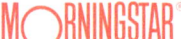

Designer: Paul Rand
*The ideal logo is simple, elegant, and timeless.
That's what I tried to do for Morningstar.* –Paul Rand

Citi: $1.5 Million in 1998[5] ($3,007,223 in 2026)

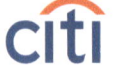

Designer: Paula Scher, Pentagram Partners
When Travelers Insurance and Citigroup merged, they wanted a new logo that honored both brands. Paula Scher famously sketched the concept on a napkin during the kick-off meeting and shared it with her partner, Michael Bierut. She recounted the story at an AIGA conference I attended in New York. The solution came quickly, because she had the experience to see it clearly. That's why they hired Pentagram.

Experienced, talented designers aren't charging for their time. They're charging for their expertise.

NEXT Computers: $100,000 in 1986[17] ($298,161 in 2026)

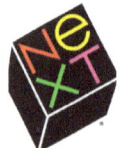

Designer: Paul Rand
Commissioned by Steve Jobs, Paul Rand famously presented the NeXT logo not in person, but through a 100-page booklet filled with process, sketches, and applications. While studying under Rand in Brissago, Switzerland, he explained to us that he preferred this approach because he did not enjoy client presentations. With his blunt Brooklyn demeanor, he just wanted to get on with the work.

According to Rand, Jobs was so pleased with the result that he insisted Rand fly to California so he could thank him in person... with a hug.

Steve Jobs was a design ambassador. He understood that design wasn't limited to a mark; it was a philosophy that should touch every aspect of the company.

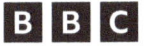

BBC (British Broadcasting Corp.)
$1.8 Million in 1997[18] ($3,664,878 in 2026)

Designer: Dalton Maag
This logo has a long history of updates and the formal use of squares first appeard in 1958. The large cost for redesign in 1997 was justified with a custom typeface.

BP (British Petroleum)
£4.6 million in 2000[19] (£8,859,600 in 2026)
Using the Bank of England's inflation calculator

Designer: Landor and Associates
Before the redesign, BP used a traditional shield with the letters "BP" inside it. They wanted to change how people perceived them, and they did.

The new logo may push the boundaries of simplicity, but it succeeded in shifting perception. It's a reminder that great design isn't always about following rules, it's about achieving the right impact for the right audience.

I Love NY: Pro Bono 1977[20]

Designer: Milton Glaser
Clearly, this logo is priceless.

Why did Glaser agree to work for free?
Because he loved New York.

Sometimes, you can appeal to the heart of a designer. If they're too busy or unable to take on a low-paying or pro-bono project, they'll let you know. But if you need branding for a meaningful mission and don't have the budget for an experienced designer, start by reaching out within your network. You might find someone whose values align with yours, and it never hurts to ask.

> **SIDE NOTE**
>
> **Marketing professionals and Copywriters**
> The famous I Love NY campaign slogan was conceived by Mary Wells Lawrence of Wells, Rich, and Greene, before Milton Glaser designed the logo. I mention this to highlight the crucial role copywriters and marketing professionals play in great design. We work best when we work together.

> "The whole purpose [of presentation] is to enable people to learn. Your mission is not to transmit information but to transform learners."
>
> — Harold Stolovitch & Erica Keeps

Chapter 7

Empowering the Client

My logo presentations are designed to empower you, not just impress you. I walk you through key parts of my process, including sketches that didn't make the cut, so you can see the thinking behind the final design. Seeing the logo in real-world applications helps you visualize its potential and impact. By the end, hopefully, you'll feel more confident recognizing what makes a logo not just good, but great.

The following example is part of a longer presentation.

Problem

The Reconnect Hungary logo was clunky, hard to read and it did not relate to the parent logo of the Hungarian Human Rights Foundation (HHRF). The logo did not match the level of professionalism that the program delivered, and the organization knew it.

When they approached me they were frustrated on a gut level. They did not know what to do, but knew they needed help.

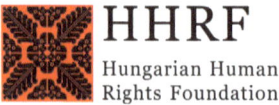 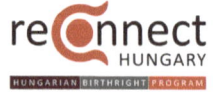

Old logo
This is a classic example of an intellectual idea that is not working formally. The designer wanted to connect the letter C with the letter O. The idea is 'connection'. The large red C and O form overwhelm the word, making it clunky. The idea is pounded into the word rather than being a subtle hint.

 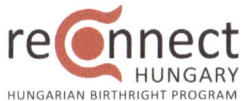

When a designer interrupts the name of the organization with a shape, as Rand did for Morningstar, it's important to be sure that the shift in the word is enough to create a unique form but not so much that legibility is hindered. In this case, the C and the O form draw too much attention. It takes away from reading the whole word.

This is a common occurrence with young designers, my-former-self included. In my early days of design the intellectual ideas were abundant but I had not yet mastered how to actually make them work. That comes with practice and experience.

Objectives
1. Relate to the long-standing HHRF logo
HHRF has a strong reputation and has been well established since 1978. The strength of the HHRF brand can help instill trust in the Reconnect Hungary program. And vice-versa, the significance of a birthright program can help keep the HHRF relevant and strong.

It was important to bring them together visually.

2. Appeal to young adults and their parents
The mark can be fresh enough to appeal to a young audience while also being professional enough to earn the trust of their parents.

Process

After a thorough exploration phase, we decided not to merely improve the form of the old logo. It was decided that a new form was needed.

When I zoomed into the HHRF logo, it seemed as if there were four arrows pointing towards the center. Could this be used somehow?

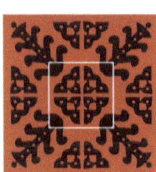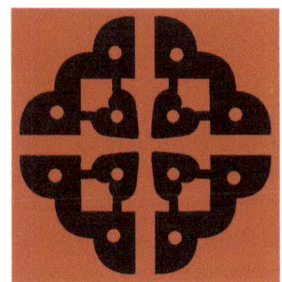

Center of the HHRF logo

This was a pleasant discovery and a great way to incorporate the mission of the project, bringing Hungarian Americans back to the homeland.

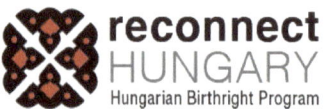

This was interesting, but not hip and young.

If I want to design logos like Saul Bass, it helps to follow his lead and make sure that the design covers the criteria established at the beginning of the project. (Saul would establish unique traits with his clients. Then he made sure the logo sketches held up to the traits.)

The logo needs to relate to the HHRF while also being hip and fresh for the young program participants.

We had to do more formal sketching. Dig deeper.

Chapter 7: Empowering the Client

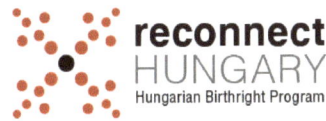

That is how we discovered the dots. We playfully explored the Hungarian folk motif of the HHRF logo and the arrows coming together.

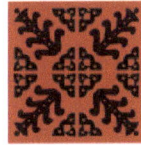

This logo hit all the client's requirements and checked my box for a strong, memorable form. I was ready to prepare the client materials.

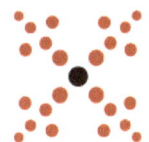

Since this logo was a form the client hadn't seen before, I sent them the presentaiton a day ahead. This gave stakeholders space to absorb it, talk it over, and approach the meeting confidently. By the time we met, they were empowered to make a clear, informed decision and the process felt smooth and collaborative.

After learning the differencc between a good logo and a bad logo, and after seeing the decision making that brought us to a final logo, the client was open to this form even though they had never seen it before and it was not what they were expecting, they embraced it

The chosen design contrasts and compliments the traditional HHRF logo. It is like wearing combat boots with a pencil skirt. It is like salt on chocolate. It is unexpected and it works.

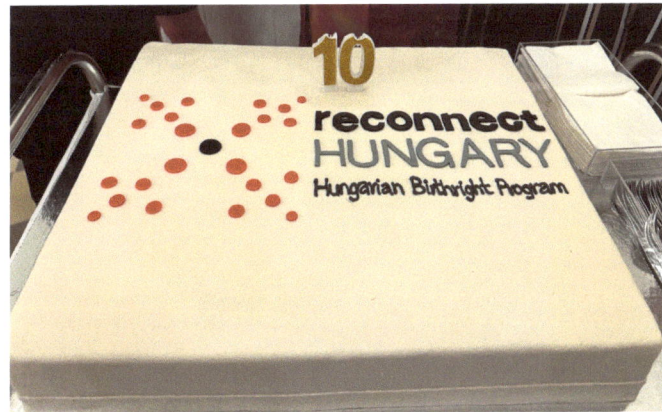

I love receiving pictures like this from happy clients. Perhaps another test for a clear logo is whether or not it can be put on a cake?

Examples of the recommended logo in action helps the client make their decision. The presentation should teach you how it will work in a real environment.

Below is a practical application.

Reconnect Hungary: First Week Itinerary July 29 - August 4, 2022

Thursday, July 29	
9:00 AM	Individual arrival at Hungarian Consulate (223 East 52nd Street, New York, NY 10022)
9:30 AM	Meet-and-Greet/Orientation at the Hungarian Consulate: language primer, Q&A, team building, lunch
9:00 AM	Departure to JFK airport Flight details: KL 1975 (KLM)

Friday, July 30	
1:20 PM	Arrival at Liszt Ferenc Airport, Budapest
2:45 PM	Check-in at Domus Collegium Hungaricum (XIV., Abonyi u. 10.) Lunch
6:00 PM	Budapest sightseeing tour by boat (Departs from Vigadó)
7:30 PM	Dinner/ Free time (settle in, exchange money, explore the neighborhood)

Saturday, July 31	
9:00 AM	Breakfast at Lion's Garden (XIV., Cházár A. u. 4.)
9:30 AM - 3:45 PM	Treasure Hunt: Discover the main attractions of Budapest
11:15 AM-12:30 PM	Visit the Hospital in the Rock (Sziklakórház) Lunch
3:45 PM	Meet at Szent István tér (V., St. Stephen's square)
4:00 - 5:00 PM	Visit St. Stephen's Basilica Free time in downtown
7:00 PM	Dinner

Sunday, August 1	
8:30 AM	Breakfast at Lion's Garden (XIV., Cházár A. u. 4.)
9:00 AM	Departure to Szentendre
10:00 AM	Visit the Skanzen (Open-Air Ethnographic Museum)
1:00 PM	Lunch at Jászárokszállás Fogadó, Skanzen
2:00 PM	Visit the Skanzen (Open-Air Ethnographic Museum) Craftwork, Walking tour in the city center of Szentendre
5:00 PM	Departure to Budapest Dinner

Monday, August 2	
8:15 AM	Breakfast at Lion's Garden (XIV., Cházár A. u. 4.)
9:00 AM-12:00 PM	Intercultural training and Hungarian language immersion (Domus Collegium Hungaricum)
12:15 PM	Lunch
4:00 PM-7:00 PM	"Walking tour in the 7th District" Visit the Dohány Street synagogue
7:00 PM	Dinner

Tuesday, August 3	
8:45 AM	Breakfast at Lion's Garden (XIV., Cházár A. u. 4.)
9:30 AM	Lecture about roma culture, history, roma integration, policy, etc. by István Forgács and Kata Kárász
12:00 PM	Lunch
12:35 PM	Departure to Kesztyűgyár
1:00 PM-2:30 PM	Visit the Kesztyűgyár (VIII. Mátyás tér 15.)
2:30 PM	Departure to Széchenyi Thermal Bath
3:00 PM-6:00 PM	Proceed to soak in the Széchenyi Thermal Baths
6:30 PM-8:30 PM	Dinner/mingle with the Locals & Informal meeting with Hungarian students, young professionals

Wednesday, August 4	
8:30 AM	Breakfast at Lion's Garden (XIV., Cházár A. u. 4.)
10:00 AM	Visit the Holocaust Memorial Center (IX., Páva utca 39.)
	Free Time See Optional Programs at the end of the Program Manual!

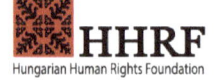
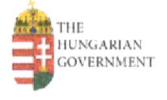

Organized by the Hungarian Human Rights Foundation and supported by the Government of Hungary.

Chapter 7: Empowering the Client

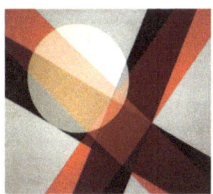

Creative use

Designing something creative and fun for each new logo helps show the potential for extended branding.

Since László Moholy-Nagy is one of my favorite artists and he was Hungarian, I decided to explore a t-shirt design inspired by his work.

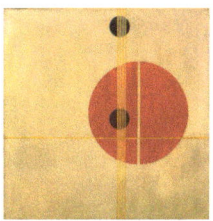

The paintings on the left are examples of Mohaly-Nagy's work. He used circles, lines and planes to create bold compositions of abstract artwork. Since the logo we recommended is an abstract mark made of circles, it seemed like a fun idea to create an abstract composition using circles while incorporating the logo and the name. It's a fresh take on a Hungarian legend.

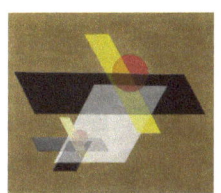

Mohaly-Nagy was a modern Hungarian artist, creating iconic work that was very different from the traditional Hungarian folk art, an appropriate homage for the fresh young brand that Reconnect Hungary was looking for.

As seen on page 55, the new logo was embraced by the Hungarian Human Rights Foundation. Putting the logo onto a cake says 'success'.

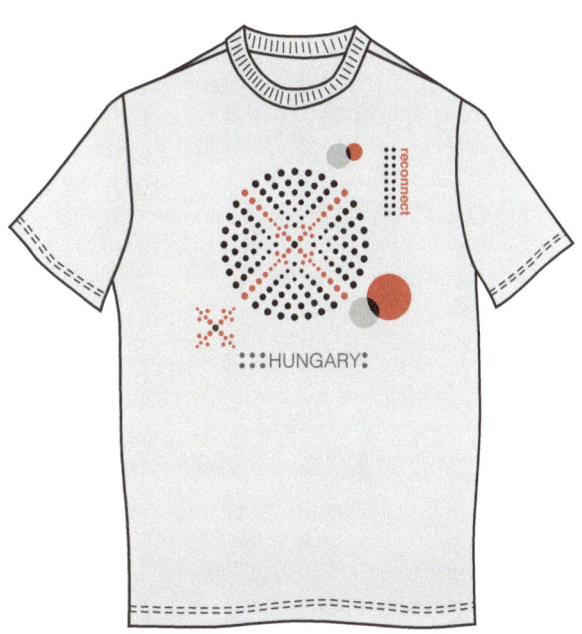

57

> "The biggest mistake a small business can make is to think like a small business."
>
> — Aruna Bhayana

Conclusion

Finding Soul in Simplicity

After more than 20 years as a designer, I've developed a deep passion for logo design. In today's world, it's easy to buy a logo for $100 or less. But a logo isn't just a graphic, it's the foundation of your brand. Savvy business leaders know that investing in thoughtful design signals the quality of their product or service and sets them apart from the competition.

It really does say that you care.

Timeless logos are priceless.

In 1995 I was fortunate enough to take a course taught by Paul Rand. One of the many things I learned was the importance of being playful and human during your process, not intellectualizing everything. Rand pushed us to explore form in an effort to find the unexpected. He wanted us to let go, allow our hands and heart to work without the mind being too overbearing. We must think, but not over-think. Let our hearts lead the work. Feel the form. His passion was both intimidating and contagious.

Finding soul in simplicity has become my mantra. This type of work requires a human heart. I hope that my experience can help you be a design ambassador and take your business to higher levels.

Good design is good will.

chickadeefly.com
linkedin.com/in/loreleidanilchick/

Gratitude

Mom and Dad
Thank you for fueling me with blind confidence, a trait that has led to fun adventures and purposeful work.

Celia Doremus
Copy editor extraordinaire and good friend.

Ken Pasternak
Honest friend and sharp critic.

Nancy and Scott Aaron
Thank you for encouraging me to write this book.

Karen Klami
When this book was just an idea, I mentioned it to my stylist. A woman across the salon chimed in, "I love that idea!" That woman was Karen, who became my cheerleader. No charge, no pressure, just one woman supporting another.

Vince and Carla
When I left Boston's vibrant AIGA community and moved to Vermont, I was lucky Vince and Carla made the move too. We traded design lectures for snowboarding, and their team at Boss Office Works has been a constant source of print and design support.

Anna, Cyrille, Eduardo, Fernanda, Lorena, Lucinda, Marc, Melissa, Michelle & Nicola
I'm forever grateful for creative friends who are living their best creative lives and inspiring me to do the same.

Brenda, Elisa, Heather, Jenna, Kimmy, Michele & Rita
You inspire me every day.

Special thanks to Heather for reading my first draft and Kimmy for editing my final draft.

Ted, Adelle, Theo and Darla
This book took two years longer than planned, thanks to my family. Honestly, you're just too fun to ignore, and way harder to edit.

Thank you.

Endnotes

1. *The Power of a Good Logo*, MIT Sloan School of Management
   sloanreview.mit.edu/article/the-power-of-a-good-logo/
2. *Design, Form and Chaos,* Paul Rand
3. *Designing Brand Identity* by Alina Wheeler: logo catagories
4. shell.com/who-we-are/our-history/our-brand-history.html
5. Scher, Paula. Interview by Debbie Millman. Design Matters. April 9, 2007. designobserver.com
   (Paula Scher states that the Citi rebrand was priced at $1.5 million, including the logo designed by her at Pentagram.)
6. coca-cola.com/gb/en/media-center/coca-cola-logo-media-center and creativebloq.com/news/coca-cola-logo-history
7. inkbotdesign.com/gap-logo-design/
8. audi-mediacenter.com/en/press-releases/double-debut-in-shanghai-audi-and-the-audi-e-concept-16359
9. about.att.com/innovation/ip/brands/history
   Design history: logohistories.com/p/logo-design-saul-bass-bell
10. virgin.com/about-virgin/latest/the-evolution-of-the-virgin-logo
11. cropink.com/logo-statistics
    article by Manisha Saini, Data Driven Marketing Expert
12. copyright.gov/ai/Copyright-and-Artificial-Intelligence-Part-2-Copyrightability-Report.pdf
13. Content Marketing Institute, 2015
14. CurateLabs.co, Sept 2024
16. Heller, Steven. Paul Rand. New York: Phaidon Press, 2000.
    (Documents that Paul Rand was paid $50,000 in 1981 to design the Morningstar logo.)
17. Jobs, Steve. Steve Jobs: The Lost Interview.
    Directed by Paul Sen. Triumph Media, 2011.
    (Steve Jobs confirms that Paul Rand was paid $100,000 to design the NeXT logo in the 1980s.)
18. BBC News. "BBC Defends £1.15m Logo." BBC News, July 2, 1997. news.bbc.co.uk/2/hi/uk_news/385409.stm
    (Reports the BBC paid £1.15 million for its 1997 logo redesign by Lambie-Nairn. Some sources later cite £1.8 million for full rollout.)
19. Elliott, Stuart. "Rebranding BP." The New York Times, June 11, 2001.
    nytimes.com/2001/06/11/business/media-rebranding-bp.html
    (Reports that Landor Associates was paid £4.6 million for the BP Helios logo, part of a $211 million global rebranding.)
20. Glaser, Milton. Interview by Chip Kidd. "Design Matters".
    February 8, 2005. https://designobserver.com
    (Milton Glaser confirms he created the I Love NY logo pro bono in 1977, without compensation.)
    Also in: The New York Times, "Milton Glaser, Influential Graphic Designer, Dies at 91," June 26, 2020.

www.ingramcontent.com/pod-product-compliance
Lightning Source LLC
Chambersburg PA
CBHW040322220526
45473CB00009B/2528